Is Your House OVERWEIGHT?

Recipes for Low-Fat Rooms

ARHAUS

Is Your House Overweight?

Sharon Kreighbaum

Heather Lane Publishing
Hudson, OH

Published by Heather Lane Publishing, Hudson, Ohio.

Heather Lane Publishing is a division of Heather Lane Properties.

Library of Congress Cataloging-in-Publication Data 2011927585
Kreighbaum, Sharon

Is Your House Overweight? Recipes For Low-Fat Rooms / Sharon Kreighbaum

ISBN 978-0-9846436-0-8

Editing and Book Layout by Richard Lucas, Dancing Tornado Design
Graphics by Richard Lucas, Dancing Tornado Design
Illustrations (including cover) by Justin Campbell
Vintage props provided by Joe Valenti
Vintage prop photography and author headshot by Linda Ford, Linda's Lenses
Room photography by Nicole Bartolozzi, Moments By Cole Photography

Dedication

To the sentimental saver, misdirected collector, and project procrastinator in us all.

Acknowledgments

Richard Lucas, Dancing Tornado Design, is responsible for text editing, creating retro graphics and book layout. Justin Campbell designed Barbara, Betty, and Bob, and drew all illustrations. Joe Valenti, Flower Child, provided all vintage props. Nicole Bartolozzi, Moments By Cole Photography, shot the before and after room photos, and Linda Ford, Linda's Lenses, shot the photographs of the vintage props and author headshot.

Special Thanks

To Marge Hogan Mackey for her expertise as a professional organizer.

Table of Contents

Introduction

Overweight houses have become an epidemic - stuff overflowing into rarely-used rooms and then into storage units. The storage rental business is booming. People would rather store stuff than declutter.

If you find your house to be overweight, there is hope. Your house will lose pounds and inches when you put it on a diet. Even if your house isn't obese, this book can help it lose that last 10 pounds.

I have three passions in life: glamour, efficiency, and comfort. In this book I'll deal with all three and how they directly influence the way your house looks, works, and accumulates stuff.

Since the Great Depression, people have been keeping objects for fear of being without. The "it might come in handy someday" school of thought encouraged us to keep things just in case.

A generation later, the 1950's became an era where household goods were manufactured with longevity in mind. Things were made to last. Today they become obsolete because technology changes so fast. Some of us, however, continue to keep things that are past their prime – no longer used, loved, or needed.

The 1950's was a time when homes provided a sense of peace, warmth, and order. Styles were uncluttered, beautiful, comfy, clean, welcoming, and well-organized. Fashions were glamorous. Women wore dresses, hats, gloves, and high heels. Men wore suits, hats, and wing-tipped shoes. Life seemed more glamorous, yet wonderfully simple and organized at the same time.

I've chosen three characters that will help illustrate ways you can make your own house more simple, organized, and, yes, even glamorous. Have fun with Barbara, Betty, and Bob as they share with you their views, stories, and suggestions. I think you'll like them. They're a fun bunch.

When you take this book to heart, it will instill in you a discerning and generous lifestyle to encourage evaluating your things for the purpose of sharing them with others. As a result, your house will not only lose the weight but keep it off.

Part One

Meet the Characters

Dear Reader,

Since you'll be reading my advice throughout this book, I'll describe myself so you know where I'm coming from. I appreciate beauty and cherish my relationships with others. I prefer hanging out with men because they have better stories. When I'm at a party and a woman starts talking about her kids, I leave to refresh my drink, usually a martini.

My ideal house is one that is glamorous, comfortable, and set up for entertaining. I'd love to call "sensual" but people take it wrong. A house should please the five senses – sight (look fabulous), smell (cinnamon rolls baking in the oven), touch (cashmere blanket, Egyptian sheets), sound (Dean Martin, Frank Sinatra, Tony Bennett, Nat King Cole), and taste (chocolate in the candy dish).

I'm passionate about having people over for dinner parties. It gives me an excuse to wear a gown. When people ask why the gown, I reply, "I didn't dress for this party, darling, I dressed for the one I'm going to next." My house also gets thoroughly cleaned. If you want a really clean house, invite people over. I don't hesitate to rearrange the furniture, switching it from room to room. Since I have parties often, Helen Keller could never live here.

Everyone likes to hang out in the kitchen, so the sofa and chairs go to the kitchenette to make room for the dining table in the family room. A fire in the fireplace and live piano music makes for great atmosphere. I hire young, good-looking music majors (guys of course) from the local college to play the piano. Some look so good they become the room's focal point.

When it comes to designing people's homes, I spend time with the clients to determine their passions – how they live and what they love. It's fascinating to see how people live – much better than just driving by random homes at night looking into lighted windows.

I love to read murder mysteries and look at gorgeous men. My favorite color is red, my favorite spectator sport is football (so much testosterone squeezed into tight uniforms), my favorite lawn ornament is a pink flamingo, and my favorite food is anything Italian.

Love,

Barbara

Dear Reader,

I'm going to help you develop a clean, spacious, and organized home. I'm an efficiency expert, so here's what I want you to do: get rid of everything you don't use regularly. When going through each room, make rapid-fire decisions like a nurse in a busy emergency room. Then we can talk about putting the rest in a permanent place, where you'll use it most.

Having every room fully functional for specific activities is my focus. When you keep only what you use, where you use it, you'll experience less stress. You won't be frantically searching when you need something. Much less time will be wasted, and cleanup will be quick and easy.

I'm a proponent of speed clearing and speed cleaning. I like to save money, clean with all-natural, homemade products already found in the kitchen or laundry, and recycle everything.

My favorite people are engineers who develop highly-efficient spaces (airplanes, ships, submarines, RV's). My favorite food is organic vegan. My favorite exercise is Yoga. My favorite decorating style is mid-century modern, and my favorite pastime is watching a doorman in New York City hail cabs.

With a doorman, not a second is wasted. As a steady stream of guests exit a building, he is whistling and directing the cabs to the curb. In one fluid motion, using eye contact and body language (the whistle remains in his mouth), he gets everyone, in order of appearance, into a cab that takes off as another pulls up. I'm always in awe at the orderliness and speed of this continuous movement of humanity.

My challenge for you: put your house on the Staged Makeovers Diet using the Recipes for Low-Fat Rooms. I guarantee you'll be pleased with the result.

Sincerely,
Betty

A Mouse in the House

- Meet Bob -

Dear Reader,

House diet. Great concept. People need to wake up and smell the coffee. There are a lot of overweight houses out there. You know, they have excess baggage, a spare tire or two. They need to shed some pounds.

Before I go on, let me introduce myself. My real name is Bob, but I go by Squeaky Clean. I'm a clean freak. Love to clean out, repurpose, and recycle. I work out. I eat whatever I can get my paws on, but I don't overeat. I move a lot so I don't accumulate stuff.

As I said, I'm into recycling and repurposing unused stuff, and there's lots of that in every house. In fact, I'm quite resourceful - thread spool for a dining table, thimbles for chairs, etc. I help myself to stuff people keep around but they never miss any of it. People live with a plethora of unused stuff. I never get bored because there's so much of it to check out.

I've experienced quite a few adventures, like the time I came across Tupperware - cool containers, lightweight, portable. I took a small one (no one ever missed it) to use as a hot tub. I put it under the kitchen sink that leaked to fill it with water. Then, after eating my fill from the bag of beans that I gnawed open, I got in. The gas from the beans made the bubbles, and there you go.

Or the time I made a memory quilt from pieces of underwear. I only chewed out the stained ones and the ones with holes. Again, no one noticed, and now I have a colorful quilt to keep me warm in the winter.

I get the most thrills from what people call the "junk drawer." My heart beats faster, and I get that tingly excitement of anticipation when I stumble across one. It's a treasure trove of anything and everything you can think of:
- Paperclips to make curtain rods.
- Gum wrappers to line my drawers (smell great).
- Papers galore to shred for my bedding.
- Gumball-sized bouncy ball I use for ab crunches.
- Dimes I use as dinner plates.
- Straight pins as kabob skewers.

I could go on and on. It's unbelievable the stuff people never use but keep around the house.

Pet peeves of mine? 1) Cat hair - there's nothing more disgusting than finding a cat hair in my food. 2) Moth Balls - they are so t-o-x-i-c and smell horrible. It's like living in a solvent factory next to a sewage plant downwind from a cattle ranch. Like there's really going to be a moth plague in this lifetime. I've explored every nook and cranny of many a house and never met a moth yet. 3) Mouse traps - is a piece of cheese or peanut butter worth risking my life? I don't think so. I'm having too much fun. So much to see. So much to do.

You should join me. It's fun going through stuff that's neglected, never used. Each room is a new adventure.

Get into recycling. Get into repurposing. Clear out. Clean out. -- And put your house on the Staged Makeovers Diet!!

Respectfully Yours, Squeaky Clean

Part Two

The Staged Makeovers Diet

Reduce

Repurpose

Recycle

FOR OVERWEIGHT HOUSES

The Staged Makeovers Diet: Reduce, Repurpose, Recycle

Just as people feel better when they lose weight, you will feel better when your house loses weight. When you get rid of unnecessary things you will have less to store, clean, and keep track of. Barbara says, "Love it, live with it, then let it go."

The Staged Makeovers Diet focuses on purging - getting stuff out of your system, out of your house, and out of your life. Betty's purpose is to help you efficiently redesign your home by decluttering/deleting/recycling, then repurposing/organizing/creating a home for everything you own.

When you delete and recycle you give to:

- Yourself - space.
- Others - items they need.
- The planet - sustainability.

When you get in the habit of living this way, you naturally become a more discerning shopper, and clutter does not continue to accumulate. You think twice before purchasing something because you have to consider where to put it and subconsciously ask yourself if you really need it. You stop buying duplicates and curb impulse purchases as well.

Betty: "It's freeing to eliminate the time, energy, and money associated with purchasing more items."

Barbara had a client who was a wealthy widow. She was elderly, and most of her friends had passed away. She spent her time watching TV most of the day and night and was drawn to the shopping network. She ordered items she thought might be useful someday, others that someone might eventually want, or just things that could be given as gifts. When Barbara visited her home and opened a bedroom door, she was amazed at the stacks and stacks of unopened boxes. An entire room of impulse purchases!

This is a perfect example of advertisers and manufacturers selling us on why we need their products. Learn to evaluate every sales pitch to find the reason you don't need it. For example, when looking at a kitchen chopper, say to yourself, "I have a knife that can do the job."

When you put your house on a diet you will save money by:

- Having items easily found when needed, avoiding duplicate purchases.
- Learning how to evaluate every room's function and how to use what you already own to maximize efficiency.
- Learning how to delete by establishing the habit of paring down instead of buying more.
- Perusing magazines and catalogs for display, design, organizing, and repurposing ideas.
- Learning how to determine which multi-use items to keep for maximum efficiency, eliminating the gadget impulse.

Barbara remembers a few decades ago when mothers and grandmothers didn't drive. It was a challenge just to get bundles home from the market. Less items were purchased because they had to be carried home. They also had to keep a manageable and affordable balance on their store account. Only necessary, versatile, and multi-purpose items were purchased. No wonder vinegar and baking soda were used to clean and polish just about everything!

Today we drive to stores, credit cards in hand, and impulse purchase gadgets that we think will make our lives easier. Upon arriving home, we have to empty our car and find a home for everything we bought. We've lost the art of evaluating purchases based on creativity or thriftiness in order to make do with what we already have at home.

Betty: "Deleting the unnecessary provides room for specific places where items can always be found, a permanent home. Keeping items housed where they will be needed and regularly used is key."

Emptying the dishwasher is less of a chore when you house the dishes, flatware, and glassware within reach. Paring down to what is used daily at an arm's reach is most desirable and efficient. Don't fill accessible cabinets and drawers with special occasion and seldom-used items. Their homes should be more remote (upper cabinets, top shelves, pantry, or basement).

Why create a permanent home for items? Because you can find them immediately and don't have to make a new decision every time you clean as to where to put them. Take the stress out of trying to remember. Assign a convenient, permanent home for everything you own.

Betty: "Don't wait until someone dies to go through things. Do it now so you can better utilize the extra space. Don't wait until you move to clean out and spruce up. Do it now so you can enjoy your house at its best."

How to evaluate each room:

1. Determine what activities occur in each room.
2. Consider each piece of furniture/art/accessory, and ask if it is necessary for that room's activities.
3. If the answer is no, determine what room is most appropriate, and find a home there.
4. Decide to recycle unneeded items (donate or discard).

Barbara: "Part of the evaluation process, when the intent is to put your house on a diet, is to objectively ask yourself: Do I need it? Do I love it? Where can I put it so it works best and looks great?"

Quick weight loss and cost savings can be experienced when you:

- Cancel magazine or newspaper subscriptions. You can read magazines at the library and newspapers online.
- Open all mail over a trash can.
- Donate books to the library.
- Store only catalogs you order from, throwing away the old one when a new one arrives.
- Sign up for automatic bill paying when available, and pay the remainder of bills online.

Betty: "Just as a successful food diet has to become a lifestyle, a house diet is no different. Put into practice evaluating the need, usefulness, and storage of what you own, and then you can enjoy a cleansing, giving, orderly, and efficient lifestyle."

Make your house fit for life.

Clutter Causes

Clutter Causes, Clutter Cure

Clutter Causes:

- Impulse buying – "But it's on sale!"
- Emotional buying – retail therapy.
- Sentimentality – emotional attachment to things.
- Indecision – don't know where to put something.
- Procrastination for cleaning, organizing, filing papers.
- Can't say no to freebies – items given to you from friends, family, or promotions.
- An addiction to collecting.
- Fear that if you get rid of something you will need it some day.

What Clutter Does:

Keeps us feeling defeated, tired, depressed, and guilty.

What Clutter Says:

Our stuff, whether an abundance of it, or lack of it, tells others a great deal about our personality.

A kitchen with miscellaneous items from all over the house covering every counter surface tells others that we postpone decisions, have not organized a home for everything, put off returning things, don't feel good enough about ourselves to keep the kitchen clean, and that we resort to eating out or ordering in rather than cooking at home.

A kitchen with clear countertops (no mixer, blender, toaster, canisters, paper towel holder, knife block, papers, cup of pens and pencils, phone chargers, soap containers, etc.) tells others we have found a convenient home for all our regularly-used objects and that we like to have open space to make it easier to clean, cook, serve, entertain, and pursue new projects.

People can learn so much about us by:

- What we choose to hang on our walls or keep on surfaces.
- Our furniture, which is either unique to our personality, looks like a museum, or has no specific definition.
- The type of books, CDs, and DVDs we own and whether we alphabetize them, stack them randomly, or leave them scattered about.
- The organization and cleanliness of not only our rooms, but storage in cabinets, closets, basement, attic, garage, sheds, and off-site storage facilities.

- Our car and if it's clean inside and out.
- Our appearance - clothes, accessories, jewelry/makeup (or lack of), and shoes.

These observations tell others more about our personality than spending time talking with us. We can spin conversation to impress others, but when they see our appearance, home, and car, they get the raw truth – the skinny on who we are, how we feel, what we love, and how we live.

Clutter Cure:

1. Admit you need to change.
2. Dream about your house being clean, orderly, tranquil, and beautiful.
3. Put your house on the Staged Makeovers Diet.
4. Act now.

If we reduce clutter and organize what we need and love into permanent homes we will simplify our life.

The Staged Makeovers Diet will teach you to live like you're on vacation, adopt the principle that less is more, and to share with others. If you make the diet a habit and embark on a lifestyle of recycling and giving, then you, your home, your car, and your office will all look great, which, in turn, will make you feel great.

The Buddy System: Declutter with a friend. Objectivity is priceless and can encourage you to keep going.

Let's get ORGANIZED

What keeps people from organizing their home?

- Feeling overwhelmed and not knowing where to start.
- Don't want to tackle it alone because they're afraid to make decisions that might affect others.
- Don't want to take the time - would rather be doing just about anything else.

When deciding to organize, many describe their clutter situation as, "I have too much stuff and too little space."

Usually it's not as much a storage problem as it is a purging problem. Let's get rid of unnecessary stuff first, and you'll have plenty of room for an organized storage plan. The result: you'll be able to find everything, save money by not buying duplicates, and spend less time cleaning.

This book is not about organizing your clutter. It's about dieting and deleting your clutter. Organizing on a diet is getting rid of everything FIRST, then finding the best home for the rest.

Why is it so important to get rid of everything you don't want or need before you organize? For some people, buying organizing containers is just another excuse to shop with the hope that the new system will make their life easier. Unfortunately, it can add to the clutter or encourage you to keep clutter.

It's OK to have empty space. It provides an opportunity for something new to enter your life. Notice in the after photos of the exercise room and basement in the section, "The Result at a Glance." You'll see empty shelves along the walls, and that's a good thing.

Imagine stagnant energy caused by clutter as gnats flying around your house. In October of 2007 the Cleveland Indians played at home against the New York Yankees. At game time the stadium, located off the lake, was inundated by hordes of gnats which swarmed around the players. The Yankees' pitcher and batters were so distracted by the pests they lost the game. The following day's headline in Cleveland, celebrating the underdog win, read, *Gnat In Our House!*

What should you say to clutter? NOT IN MY HOUSE.

Here's the plan:

1. Get four laundry baskets or boxes and mark them:
    A) KEEP in this room.
    B) MOVE to another room.
    C) THROW AWAY.
    D) DONATE.
2. Take everything out of the room, including furniture, art, and accessories. (This is the time to make repairs and paint if needed.)

3. Quickly evaluate each item and place in one of the four containers. Furniture, art, and some accessories may be too large so just put a note with your decision on them.
4. Now rethink how you ideally use the room. Determine the best furniture placement, and put only those items back that you love and will suit that room's activity.
5. Replace the art and accessories that you love and still serve your needs.
6. If small items (like DVDs, books, toys, etc.) are to remain, find appropriate storage containers, and assign them a permanent new home in the room. This facilitates the cleaning process and allows everyone to put things away in the same place every time.
7. Put all donations in the car or call if there are large pieces of furniture to be picked up.
8. Throw away discarded items. Be brave. If they're not worth donating, it's OK to put them in the trash or recycle bin. You don't need or want them anymore. You'll feel lighter and cleaner and so will each room.
9. Store things in bins/baskets/boxes on shelves or in cabinets, labeling each container. Remember: keep like things together, and locate where they are used most.

It truly is as easy as that. If you want to go into more detail about specific organizing activities, go to the library, and check out books on the subject.

NYLINT
ROAD BUILDERS
DUMP
ERTL

BROUGHT TO YOU IN CRISP & BRIGHT Clean-O-Vision

MUST BE SEEN
TO BE
BELIEVED!!

An EARTHQUAKE SURVIVOR'S TALE

The Exciting Story of a

YOUNG WOMAN

MAKING IT ON HER OWN WITHOUT HER

CLUTTER

SHOCKING!

AND HER LIFE IS BETTER!!

Earthquake Survivor

Sometimes it takes a disaster to make us realize that having stuff isn't all it's cracked up to be. Here is Geri's story:

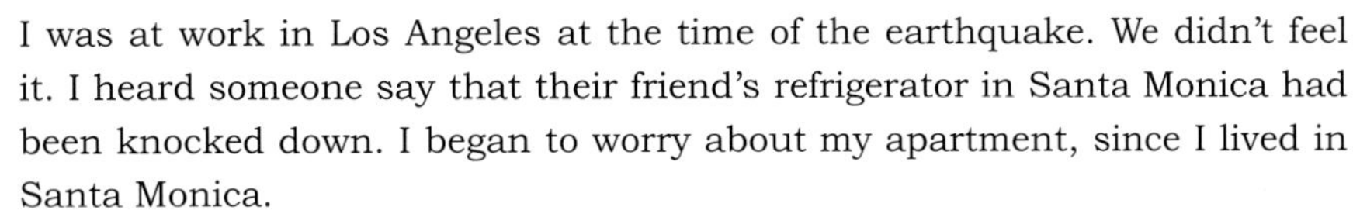

I was at work in Los Angeles at the time of the earthquake. We didn't feel it. I heard someone say that their friend's refrigerator in Santa Monica had been knocked down. I began to worry about my apartment, since I lived in Santa Monica.

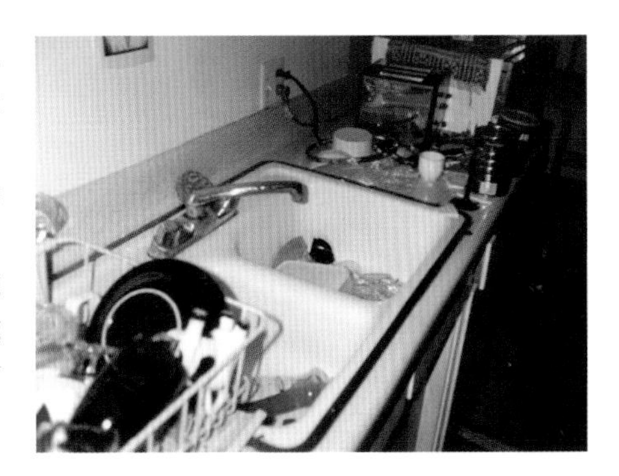

Upon arriving home, I unlocked the door but had trouble opening it because the door itself had shifted. When I was finally able to push it open, my jaw dropped at the sight. I was in shock. Free-standing cabinets had turned over, everything spilling out onto the floor. Stationary cabinets and drawers were all open.

Everything that was thrown to the floor was further destroyed by the continuous and relentless movement from the tremors. Fortunately, I found my camera undamaged and began to take pictures.

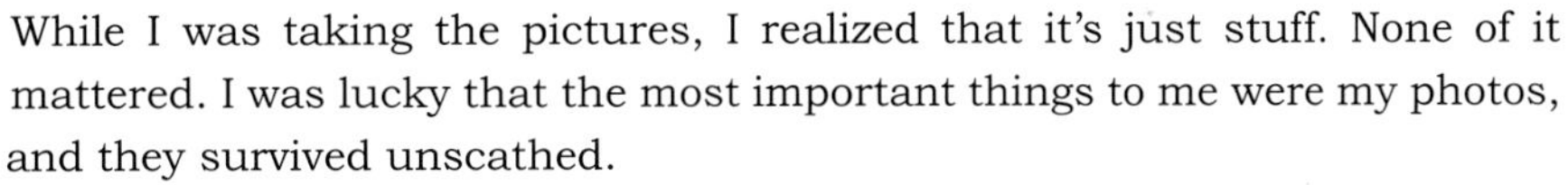

While I was taking the pictures, I realized that it's just stuff. None of it mattered. I was lucky that the most important things to me were my photos, and they survived unscathed.

I threw away everything that was broken and didn't replace it. I had more than I needed and felt I could live with much less. The city of Santa Monica is situated on a fault, so it's likely to happen again. It made me aware that I could lose more possessions in subsequent earthquakes, so I decided it was not important to replace what I had lost.

The aftershocks were unexpected and scary. If I had been in the apartment when it happened, I would have moved back to Pennsylvania.

Now my apartment is definitely less cluttered. It feels good to know that even though most of my friends have the expense of a cleaning lady, I do not. It takes me no time at all to clean!

HOW MANY

DO YOU REALLY NEED?

USUALLY NOT MORE THAN: 1

Extra, Extra – How Many Do You Really Need?

BOXES

Some of us keep boxes from every item shipped to us. Some of us keep boxes of electronic equipment and small appliances in case an item needs to be returned. Some of us do both. Save electronics boxes for 6-12 months or for the length of the warranty. When the warranty is up, get rid of the box. Any longer and the equipment becomes obsolete, and more expensive to ship and repair than to replace.

Betty encourages recycling. She feels it's OK to keep boxes to reuse for gifts, storage, an eminent move, or to ship something else. Don't save boxes for a move that may never happen. When you do move, purchase high-quality, sturdy boxes for kitchen items and anything heavy. If you reuse boxes obtained free from the grocery store, egg boxes are best. To store boxes and maximize space, cut the taped or glued seams and fold flat.

Refrain from storing items in original packaging. When Barbara remodeled a client's basement she found a sealed box containing a casserole dish. The client had never used it, didn't remember she owned it, and wouldn't be inclined to use it in the future unless it was "unpacked" and stored in her kitchen.

She also found electric rollers with the receipt taped to the box. Keep in mind it was found in the basement in storage. The receipt was from 1998. That's over a decade in storage because it was never opened and put where it could be used (bathroom).

BAGS

Plastic grocery bags can be kept to line small trash cans and to collect and discard pet waste. Keeping more than a week's worth is unnecessary as most of us shop for groceries at least weekly. Department and specialty store handled paper bags are good to keep on hand for donating items. A low-fat house would keep only as many as can be stored in a small basket.

TUPPERWARE OR OTHER STORAGE CONTAINERS

In the section, "Live Like You're On Vacation," I address this issue under the heading, "Things you can live without." We can all get by on just enough containers to store fresh food and leftovers for a week.

Betty: "After a week you shouldn't be eating the food anyway – the nutritional element is gone."

LINENS

A low-fat house has one set of sheets for each bed, sleeper sofa, or inflatable bed, a few extra pillows and blankets for guests, no more than 5 seasonal table cloths, cloth napkins for seasonal meals, 2 washcloths and bath/hand/beach towels for each family member, a few sets for guests, 2 hand towels for each bathroom, and no more than 7 dish towels and/or dish cloths.

PILLOWS

The number of bed pillows varies from person to person. To be on the safe side, plan on 2 bed pillows for each family member and have a few on hand for guests. Decorative throw pillows on the bed just prolong the time it takes to make the bed and usually end up thrown on the floor at night. If you just can't resist a beautiful pillow, use them on sofas where they will be seen more and can be useful for daytime napping.

Betty: "A low-fat house has only the number of pillows on each bed for a comfortable sleep and a few on sofas for accessorizing."

CLOTHES & SHOES

Most of us have more than we wear. I'm sure you've heard it said that we wear 20% of our wardrobe 80% of the time. Eliminate everything that you haven't worn in 6 months, needs mending, doesn't fit, or doesn't look good (not your color or current style). Keep a donation bag or box in each closet so you can routinely thin out what you no longer want.

STUFFED ANIMALS, TOYS, & GAMES

Kids hate to part with toys even if they don't play with them anymore. Emotional attachments develop from pleasurable memories. Neglected toys, games, and stuffed animals, however, can brighten the life of a needy child. Instill the character quality of generosity by encouraging kids to donate.

BOOKS, MAGAZINES, & NEWSPAPERS

Magazines and newspapers have dated material that can be found on the internet when needed. Magazines are mostly advertisements. If you feel compelled to keep an article or picture, tear out the page, and file it where you can find it again. Recycle newspapers daily as the content expires almost as soon as it is read.

Books are harder to part with, especially if they are hardcovers. Keep the ones you enjoy reading over and over or use as a reference. Share the rest with others once you have finished reading them. Truly low-fat houses have a minimum of children and adult storybooks/novels, cookbooks, and reference books. The rest can be found in the library.

TOOLS

This can be a touchy subject for the man of the house who sees a need for every tool he owns. Some have several tools of the same kind and refuse to part with any of them. It's not just tools either. There's an abundance of garages and basements overflowing with nuts, bolts, and other odds and ends that don't fit anything in the house.

DUPLICATES

To avoid purchasing duplicates, Betty suggests establishing a home for everything and keeping everything in its home.

She fondly remembers a client's laundry closet. Built in above the washer and dryer were shelves identifying the iron, detergent, starch, etc. - rows and rows of labeled objects. Betty's first reaction was, "Yes, I can see that it's an iron. I don't need a label to tell me. But then I realized that it made it easier for the family to know where to put things away. She was actually a very organized homemaker. In her house you'd know if something was missing or out of place. It was a great system, and I give her credit for running an efficient household."

BULK PURCHASES

Buying in larger quantities isn't necessarily buying smart. You may pay more per ounce, but there will be no waste. A giant bottle of ketchup takes up a lot of room in the fridge and is likely to go bad before you can use it all. Bulk purchases take up space. In trying to maintain a low-fat house it's all about dropping pounds and inches and giving yourself space.

LIVE LIKE
You're
on
Vacation!

Live Like You're On Vacation

Who wouldn't like to spend more time on vacation - no cares, no worries, surrounded by nice stuff, but less stuff - less stuff to clean, less stuff to store, less stuff to move around.

To make each room like a vacation retreat, remove things:

- You don't use regularly.
- That don't belong in the room.
- You can live without.

Things we don't use regularly: At our vacation spot we're living with only things we use every day. Even vacation places that pamper us provide only what we need for comfort and enjoyment - any more than that and we wouldn't be able to relax and unwind.

Things that don't belong in the room: Vacation destinations, whether hotels, condos, resorts, bed and breakfasts or campsites, store items where they are used. Only what is needed is provided. Remember: less is more.

Things you can live without: How much Tupperware does one really need? An entire drawer or cabinet filled with assorted containers can store enough leftovers to feed a soup kitchen. Would you have enough room in your refrigerator if you filled them all at once? Most people only use a few each week. That amount should be all you need to keep on hand. Use the valuable storage space to organize and spread out the items you use on a regular basis.

Barbara and Betty stay in a condo when they vacation in Florida. The kitchen is equipped with: one large slotted spoon, one large serving spoon, one large knife for chopping, one large serrated knife for slicing, and one small paring knife for everything else, a spatula, a cutting board, can opener, blender, mixer, measuring cups and spoons, one small and one large pot, a frying pan, a cookie sheet, a 9x12 baking pan, serving bowls, plates, cups, silverware, dish towels, and soap. The counters house only the crock of utensils, leaving plenty of workspace, in other words, only what's needed to prepare and serve meals and drinks.

Bathrooms have soap, shampoo, conditioner, toilet paper, tissues, towels, hair dryer, and cleaning supplies.

Bedrooms have empty dressers to fill with only the clothes you actually wear, lamps on the night stands for reading, and enough bed pillows to be comfortable.

In the family room, the only item on the coffee table is the remote control for the wall-mounted TV, and there is enough comfortable furniture to relax with several people. Once again, less is more.

GENEROUS
Living
Means
GIVING

Generous Living Means Giving

"It's better to give than to receive." We've heard that one before. The joy of giving is perceived as a pleasurable experience. It feels good to give. It feels good to make someone else happy. It feels good to fill the needs of others.

If you truly want a low-fat house, one that keeps its weight off, then we have to make it a habit to carefully and objectively evaluate everything we own.

It has to become routine to ask ourselves, "Do I really need it?"

Then we can come to that place where we find we can help someone else if we give it away. It's really a win-win situation because we feel good about giving, and we keep our house on the diet - good for you, good for others, good for our planet. Which is actually a win-win-win, isn't it?

To keep your house from gaining even more weight, we also have to ask ourselves, "Do I really need it?" when we're tempted by TV or radio ads, sales fliers, catalogs, or impulse buys at the store.

Put it

WHERE YOU USE IT

SAME PLACE

EVERY TIME!

Put It Where You Use It – Same Place Every Time

This sounds like common sense, but how often do we misplace our car keys, sunglasses, cell phones, etc.? How easy is it to remember where you filed an important paper or put your passport?

The solution to the frustration of wasting time looking for objects is to determine a permanent home for EVERYTHING - and then to put it there right away when you are finished using it.

You will always know where to find things quickly when needed, AND it will be easier and faster to clean.

Make the storage location the place where you use the item, or, in the case of your keys, sunglasses, and phone, where they can be accessed when coming in or leaving your house.

It's as simple as that. Or is it? Ponder this:

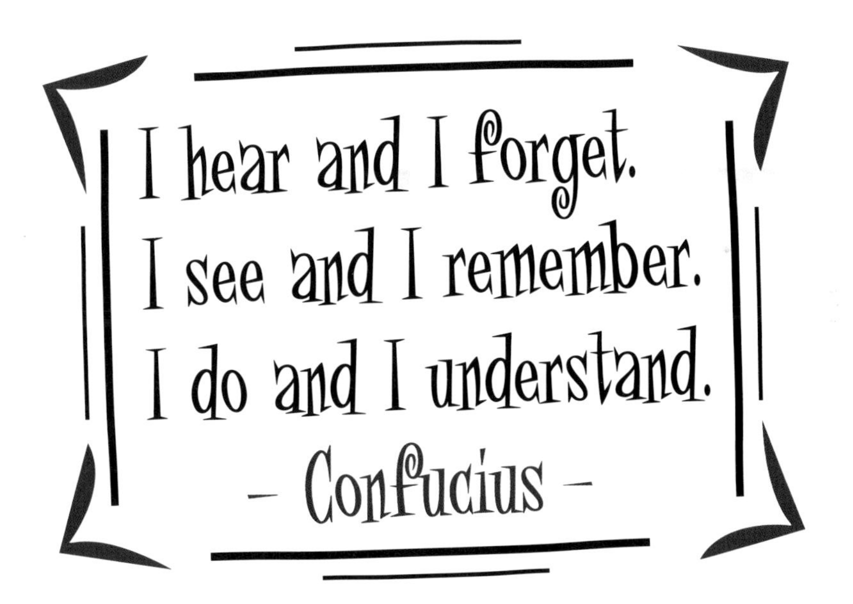

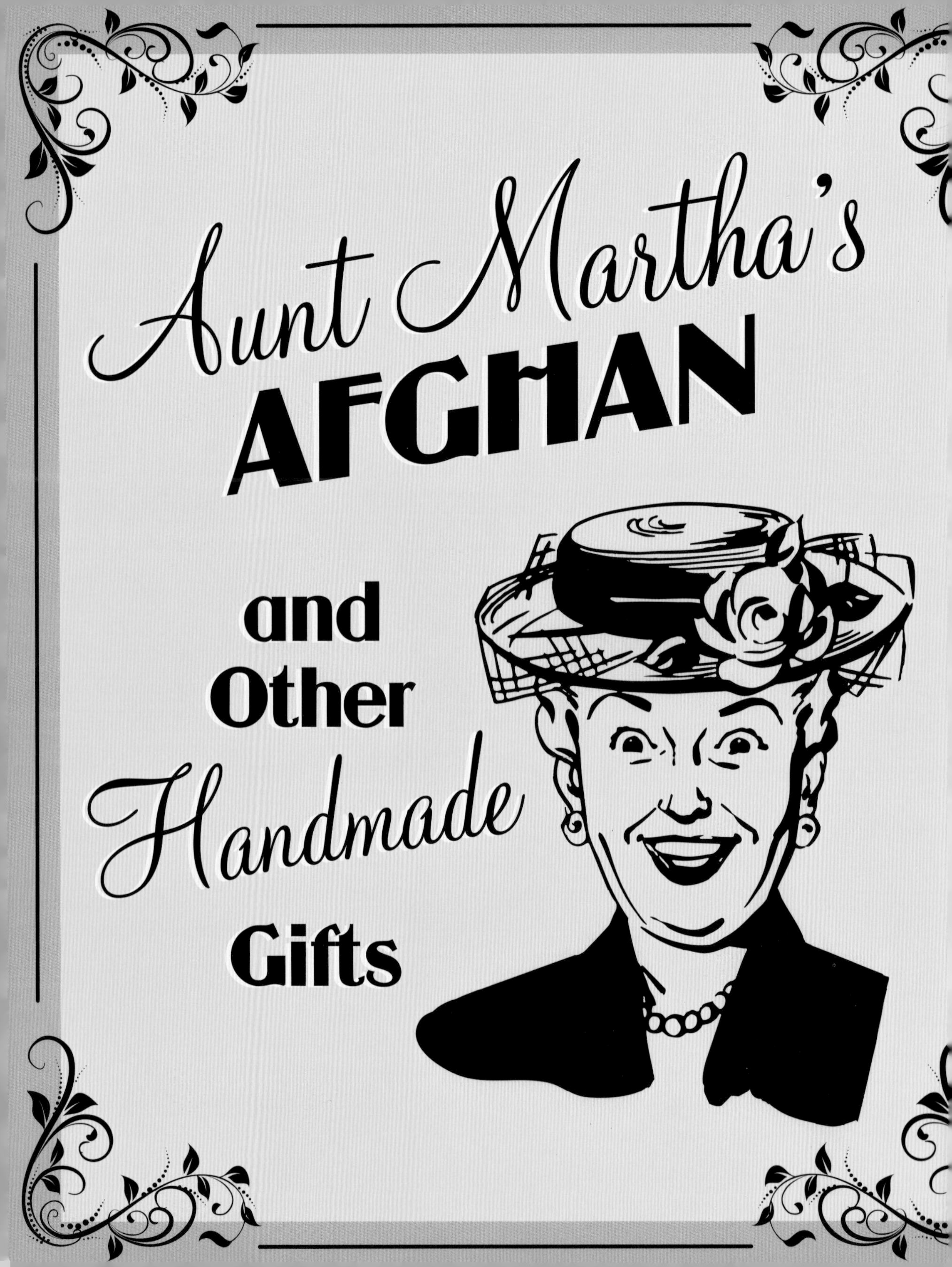
Aunt Martha's
AFGHAN
and
Other
Handmade
Gifts

Aunt Martha's Afghan and Other Handmade Gifts

A handmade gift from a loved one is hard to part with. Such thoughtfulness and hard work went into making it for you. What if you get rid of it, and then they come over to visit and notice that it's not around?

Giving a gift is a feel-good gesture for the person doing the giving. As the recipient, you can do whatever you want with the gift once it's yours. Don't feel compelled to keep it even if it's from an important person in your life. If the gift is inappropriate, doesn't fit your body, home, or lifestyle, or has served its purpose, you are free to recycle it and let the enjoyment continue with someone else.

Betty says, "To free you now, donate it, and trust that someone you don't know will enjoy its usefulness. That way you, as the giver, get to experience that feel-good gesture."

TRAVEL TRINKETS

The road to too much stuff!

Travel Trinkets – Come Home Without Them

Souvenirs - a dirty word in a low-fat house. It's fun to travel, and the memories are the best part. But we don't need souvenirs to remind us of the fun! If you shop on vacation and see a cute little ditty, take a picture of it right there in the store! The picture will fit nicely in the album with the rest of the trip.

When you come across that Hawaiian dancer statue years later you'll wonder what to do with it. You spent good money on it, but where do you put it? How can you give that away? Would you have to find someone who had been to Hawaii? Would a family member really want the clutter?

What about all the mugs, keychains, shot glasses, plastic swords, and Hello Kitty stuff? These are all well-meaning impulse buys but they don't help your house when it's on a diet.

Bring home the memories, not more stuff.

INCOMING
JUNK MAIL
You've got clutter!

LOOK OUT!
IT'S COMING TO TAKE YOUR SPACE!!

Junk Mail – A Redundancy of Words

Isn't most mail junk? So much bill paying and correspondence is done electronically now that most of the items placed in our mail box are fliers, ads, credit card applications, catalogs, magazines, etc. Everybody wants your money, and they're spending postage, and precious paper, and ink resources to try to pry it from you.

Open all your mail over a trash can. Keep only personal cards, bank/insurance/tax statements, and any stray bills that are not done electronically.

Put the bills in a place where you'll be able to pay them before the due date. Remember to assign a permanent home for bill paying.

File bank, insurance, tax statements, and miscellaneous receipts in their permanent homes.

Enjoy reading the personal cards, catalogs, and magazines. Be brutal, and throw away or recycle the cards and catalogs. I know some of you will keep the cards. If you do, put them in a box or file. Tear out pictures or articles from the magazines, and throw the rest away or recycle if appropriate.

Whew, you've tackled the mail!

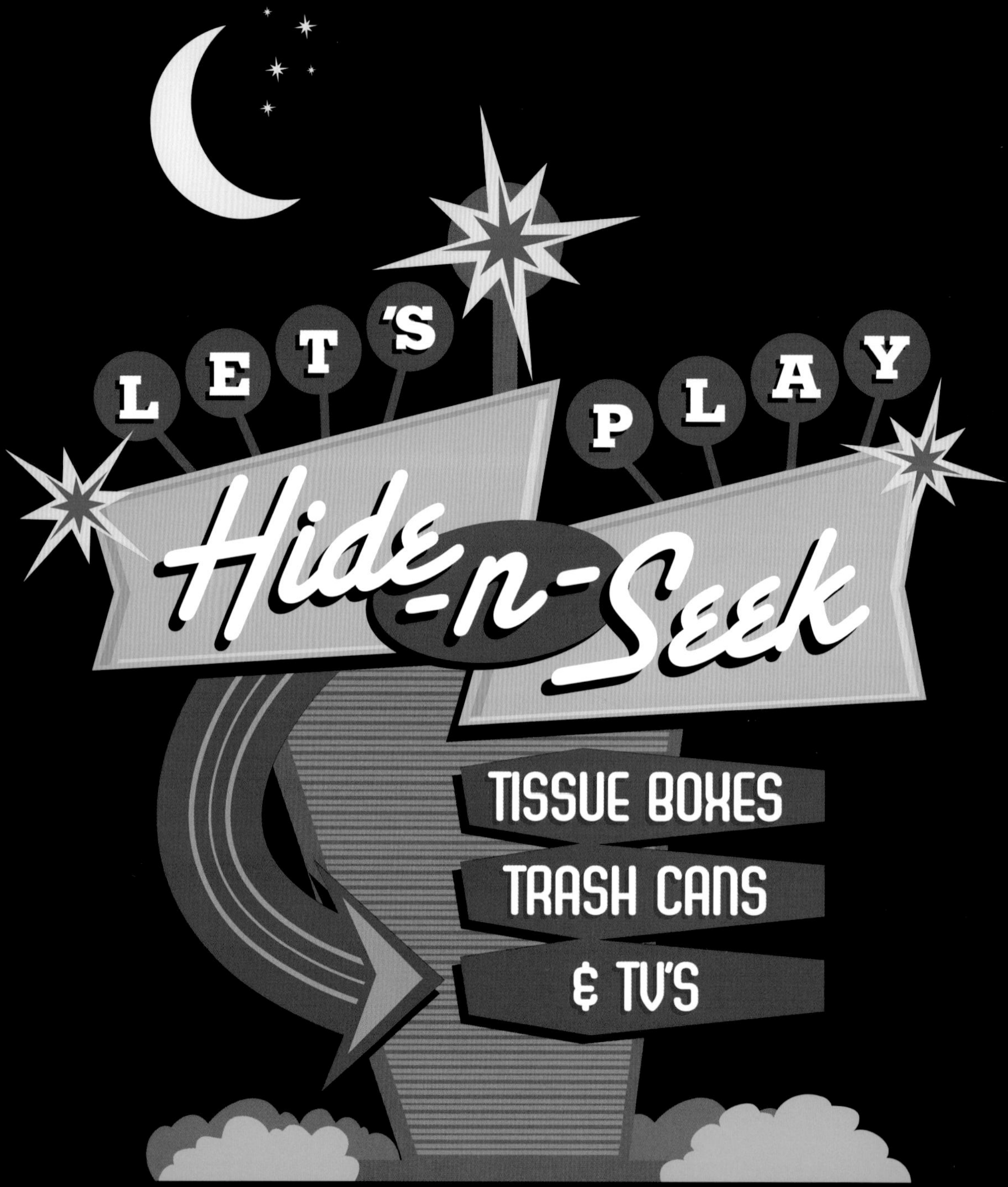

LET'S PLAY

Hide-n-Seek

TISSUE BOXES

TRASH CANS

& TV'S

Tissue Boxes, Trash Cans, & TV's – Let's Play Hide-n-Seek

Barbara: "I want to see beauty and glamour in houses. It bothers me to see tissue boxes, trash cans, and yes, even TV's, in plain sight."

Tissue boxes are unappealing and remind people of sickness. Store in cabinets, pantries, closets, or drawers. This is challenging only when suffering with allergies, a cold, or the flu.

Trash cans, even empty ones, never look good and remind people of, well, trash. They have an "unclean" aura. Keep them tucked away in cabinets, closets, or under an office desk.

Barbara: "TV's are best hidden in cabinets or entertainment centers with doors that close. I sympathize with people who have wall-mounted flat screens. I don't like to see a big, black rectangle on any wall."

The only solution here is to buy a DVD from a museum that "plays" works of art from the masters. That way you can enjoy priceless art for the actual price of a little electricity.

Indoor WEEDING

CLIP THE CLUTTER!!

Indoor Weeding

Newspapers, mail, and magazines become regular intrusions in our lives. They become indoor weeds.

Shoes, clothes, empty drinking glasses, and any other items that make their way into other rooms throughout the house are also indoor weeds.

For a quick decluttering exercise, throw everything that doesn't belong in that room into a laundry basket, and either return the items to their home or place them in the recycling or donating bin.

When decisions need to be made to donate or toss, ask yourself, "How important is that 20-year-old 3rd place bowling trophy? Am I going to read those books again? How often do I use that footstool? Why is Grandma's sewing cabinet taking up space when no one in the family sews?"

Betty: "It's amazing how much weight each room can lose when you start weeding out the unnecessary."

Don't 'Pack & Spend'!

STORAGE UNITS

STORAGE

VERY Expensive Real Estate!

Storage Units – Very Expensive Real Estate

Betty: "I've come across boxes stored in basements, attics, garages, sheds, and storage units that were sealed for years without being opened. Unless they're full of priceless memorabilia, it's obvious you don't need them to enjoy life, so why pay to store them? No matter where they're stored, they still cost you in valuable square feet of living space or a monthly storage unit expense."

Barbara tells of a client who went to her storage unit to get items for a garage sale. It was filled with old clothes, broken bikes, discarded toys, old furniture, broken lamps, and unwanted miscellaneous items. They were spending $175 per month for the past eight years (a total of $16,800) for junk that wouldn't even sell at a garage sale.

Barbara: "If they had recycled everything they would have saved $16,800 and shared with others in the process. It seems selfish to keep things you're not using. It would be great if more people were generous, recycling their extras by donating."

FAMILY

Photos

Family Photos – The Albums Have It

Barbara: "I've been in many homes where the kids are teens or grown, and there are baby photos still on the walls - and not just a few. I get it that you've spent a fortune on professional photography to capture those cute shots and another fortune on framing."

My suggestion is to take the photos out of the frames, store them in photo albums, and put a current photo, piece of art, or print in its place.

I much prefer art to photos. Photos represent a past event. The people and places change and are different today than they were yesterday. Art is timeless and beautiful.

Betty: "I always feel a bit uncomfortable when I'm in a home with an abundance of personal photos on walls and surfaces. I feel like an intruder into their family experiences."

Put away the photos, get out the art.

Celebrate the past. Enjoy the now. Dream about the future.

Collections

THEY'RE CLUTTER!

Collections

Collections are fun. They're a way to celebrate an interest with the thrill of the hunt. True collectors display their collections.

Hoarders think they're collectors but save things indiscriminately and have an inability to categorize, organize, or distinguish between trash and treasure. Their collections are not displayed, but rather stacked randomly.

The problem: when you express an interest in something like cats for instance, and everyone gives you cat-related items, such as cat magnets, cat pictures, cat plates, cat sayings, cat books, etc. It goes on and on. Even if you lose interest, well-intentioned family and friends can't resist when they see cat stuff, and they think of you.

Betty: "Even if you're a true collector and enjoy a valuable collection, you don't have to display the entire lot. Choose a select few, and rotate them occasionally. Too many of anything becomes clutter and is hard to take in all at once. A few items can be appreciated and pique a person's interest."

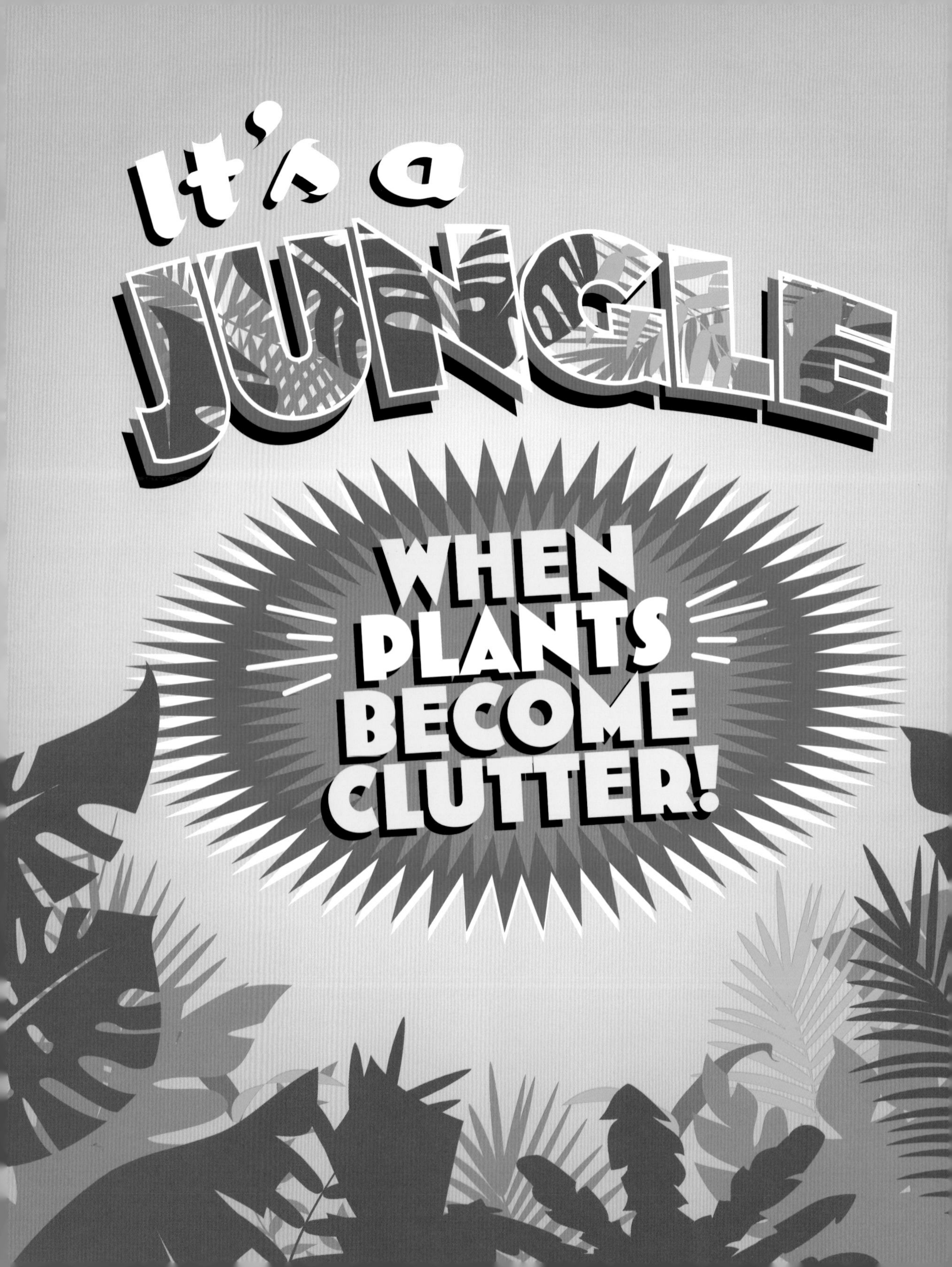
It's a
JUNGLE
WHEN
PLANTS
BECOME
CLUTTER!

It's A Jungle – When Plants Become Clutter

Indoor plants clean the air, add beauty, color, texture, and a sense of the outdoors. They are living things which are both good and bad: good because they give us oxygen and provide a benefit to our physical and emotional health, and bad because people can't part with them even when they're dying or dead.

The problems with live plants:

- Since they are living, people can't let them go.
- Too many can contribute to high humidity.
- They take up space, and too many become clutter.
- They have to be watered, fed, and placed in appropriate light and temperature settings.
- Water damage to floors and surfaces can result from water spillage and leaking containers.

Barbara: "I love live plants for balancing the ions emitted from electronic devices. I prefer to keep live plants at a minimum, however, and mix it up with artificial plants in places with low light (corners) or where watering can be difficult or damaging."

ARE *hard* TO PART WITH

Hardcovers Are Hard To Part With

Books are my weakness as I am an avid reader. It's hard to resist a sale at the library or bookstore. However, I have learned to give away books when I'm finished reading them, and regularly go through my home library for donations.

Hardcover books look great, can be used to add height on a table, and act as a sound buffer when stored on bookshelves against a wall. They also serve as welcome company on dreary, lonely days.

Having an impressive collection can be a status symbol. They can make a house feel and look homey and give the impression of unlimited learning opportunities. Books from our youth rekindle fond memories of being read to and of stimulating our imaginations.

They do, however, pose as clutter when stacked in rooms, serving as reminders that we don't have the time to get to them. Books also are, at the very least, dust collectors. This can be a significant issue in bedrooms, especially in those of children or adults that suffer from asthma or other respiratory problems.

Rooms can lose weight immediately by simply removing books. They can be found in family/living rooms, offices, bedrooms, bathrooms, and kitchens (cookbooks). In striving for low-fat rooms, keep the few books you love, know you'll refer to again, or use for decorating.

Donate books for others to enjoy. You can always go to the library if you feel you want something "new" to read.

Who's the BOSS?

Who's The Boss?

Betty: "I've been in many home offices where there were stacks and stacks of paperwork on the desk, floor, and every available surface."

Items that have no home are often relegated to the office – extra furniture, shopping bags, crafts, hobbies, ironing boards, and collectibles. People dread working there due to the clutter surrounding them.

Be the boss. Take charge. Empty the room of everything that doesn't relate to work or filing of important papers. Clear a work surface. Go through your filing cabinets every year to dispose of unnecessary paperwork. Donate duplicates. It's amazing how many staplers, tape dispensers, pencils, pens, markers, erasers, paperclips, rubber bands, etc., are found around the house, even several in the office itself.

Clutter can accumulate on a desktop or laptop as well. In decluttering, be sure to delete old files, unnecessary emails, documents, and programs that no longer serve you. In some cases it may enable your computer to run faster.

A clean, spacious, organized, and simplified office allows for concentration, imagination, and productivity.

Act like a boss, and clean house.

A Typical After-the-Purge Story...

A Typical After-The-Purge Story

You determine your house will be lighter and that you can live better without several items. You plan to give the hand mixer to your daughter because you have a Kitchenaid, donate a bunch of clothes to Goodwill, give two upholstered chairs to your son for his new condo, give craft items to your five-year-old nephew, take leftover organizing items to your mother's house next out-of-town visit, have a stack of religious books to take to the church library, another stack for the public library, a bag of magazines to the interior design department of the local university for student cut books and presentation boards, exercise and sports equipment to the local detention center, and a ton of odds and ends that you can sell at a garage sale. Now:

1. Put the hand mixer in a department store handled bag and in your car trunk. Call your daughter to let her know you're coming over.
2. Put the clothes for Goodwill in garbage bags, and place in the car trunk. Stop there after your daughter's visit.
3. Tell your son he can have the chairs if he picks them up right away.
4. Mail the craft items to your nephew. Kids love to get mail.
5. Handle-bag the organizing items for your next out-of-town visit, and put in the garage in plain sight. Then call to schedule that visit.
6. Handle-bag the books, one for the church, one for the library, and another one for the magazines. Put them in your car trunk (or back seat if the trunk is full), and plan a trip to all three places.
7. Call the detention center to set a time to pick up the sports and exercise equipment.
8. Forget about a garage sale.

Betty doesn't suggest garage sales unless you are willing to label, sort, set up tables and racks, merchandise like items together, and sit all day watching people look at your great stuff at ridiculously low prices and turn away not interested, or ask if you'll take less. You're practically giving it away as it is but you'll take it because you've decided to live without it.

Now you're faced with a dilemma: what to do with all the items that didn't sell. You've already invested about a week in the preparation and sale, and now you have to remove prices, bag all the items, and then take them to Goodwill. Even if you made $120 on the items you did sell, was that worth a week's work?

Bags and boxes of valuable stuff that you plan to sell on Craigslist or eBay can linger for weeks, months, or years. Your house won't lose the pounds and inches until they're gone. It takes a considerable amount of time photographing, pricing, downloading, and monitoring your account(s), not to mention taking calls from prospective buyers, and scheduling a time to meet for the transaction. No-shows are common. All this takes up valuable time for items that are sold at low, resale prices.

Betty's advice: "Forgo the garage sale, Craigslist, and eBay. Donate everything, get the charitable receipt, and enjoy the tax savings - less work, less time, less stress."

DIET

Part Three

Design on a Diet

Repeat After Me: Less Is More – Bigger Is Better

When you highlight only a few cherished objects in a room, they each receive attention. They're noticed, appreciated, and they become prominent. The room feels calm, spacious, clean, open, and inviting. Believe me, less is more.

Barbara's friends have an original Picasso hanging on their wall. They travel all over the world and display lots of unique items from several countries. The room is so crowded that the Picasso is overlooked. Its prominence is lost. It blends in with the other items vying for attention. Those items may be expensive as well, but certainly not as priceless as the original Picasso.

Imagine having the Picasso hanging above the fireplace all alone with no distractions. It certainly would be unforgettable to everyone entering the room.

One large piece of art or print on the wall is more dramatic, and at the same time more calming, than several small pictures. This rule holds true for items on a surface. One large vase or bowl is better than a grouping of many random items. If you must use more than one, three is a good number, but include varying heights. Use two of the same item for symmetry when flanking a large object.

Scale is important. Less is more. Bigger is better.

From the Pages of

The Clutterville Dispatch

LEFT HOOK!

Lazy Bachelor Hangs Pictures and Art on Hooks Left by Previous Tenant

Shames Family with Bad Taste

"I thought I'd brought him up better than this. Clarence has a thing or two to learn about living on his own." Those are the words of teary-eyed Elsie Wallace, mother of Clarence C. Wallace, recent graduate of Regent Technical Institute, upon first seeing the decor of his apartment in his foray into independent adult living. "You don't just hang your pictures and paintings wherever the last roomer hung his. It is disheveled, uneven, and lazy!"

DESPISED BY NEIGHBORS

"We dearly wish young Mr. Wallace had never moved into our wonderfully clean, well-maintained building," said Madeline Reinhart who lives four doors down from Wallace. "The clutter in his front room alone was so discomforting that Harold, my husband, insisted we immediately turn our welcome wagon right around," she explained, adding, "That kind of slack young man would likely let our generous gift of 12 petunias lilt away and die."

LADYFRIEND TERMINATES RELATIONSHIP

"I was so proud of Clarence after graduation. Honestly, I'd dreamt of us marrying in the future," said Wilma Hodges, Wallace's former girlfriend, "but on his own he's a different man, and I can't live with a person who has such poor taste and doesn't care about proper decor, let alone a sense of elegance about his surroundings. I look forward to and will be proud to become someone's housewife some day, but it will have to be with a man who knows how to treat his dwelling as well as he treats his lady.

Wallace, though visibly flushed with disgrace and heartache, had no comment, and did not permit photography on his premises. Let this be a lesson to us all.

Hanging Out with Art

When it comes to deciding on art, you can get inspiration and current trends from looking at magazines at doctor's offices or the library, or you can study the design of TV and movie sets, or you can tour model homes, or you can notice the details in high-end hotels, restaurants, etc.

Original art is great when you can afford it, but prints can make a big bang for the buck, especially on a budget. Be creative, and frame greeting cards and even pictures from catalogs and magazines.

Just as workers need at least one day off a week to rest, our eyes need at least one wall in a room that is "blank" to rest.

"It's a Good Size" - A Decorating Story

My good friend, Frank, was going through a difficult time. Having gone through a second divorce, he found himself moving, alone, into a modest two-bedroom apartment in West Los Angeles. He was sad and unsure about his future. But when he was all settled in, he invited my girlfriend, Maria, and me to visit for dinner and wine, and to show us how he'd proudly decorated all by himself. He was especially excited about a couch which he'd had custom upholstered.

Now, judging from Frank's conservative, out-of-date clothing and all-too-practical car, we didn't expect much of a "wow" factor. In fact, I asked Maria, "What if it's awful? He's taken a pretty tough blow, and I know he wants to impress, especially women. What do we say if we don't like it?"

"Well," she said, "We certainly can't say anything negative, but we can't be dishonest. If the couch, for example, is too awful for comment, then let's just say, 'It's a good size,' and leave it at that."

When we arrived, Frank welcomed us with a broad smile and two generous flutes of champagne. The mellow swing of Nat King Cole's voice swirled through the air along with the aroma of vanilla candles and fresh paint. The first thing we saw was the couch. You couldn't miss it. It was rounded and flourished and upholstered in cream-colored cotton with large roses. It looked like something my grandmother would have inherited from her grandmother. "Pretty stunning, don't you think? - $1,200," he said. We were stunned, indeed, into a frozen silence. Maria looked at me in a panic.

"...It's... It's... It's a good size," I mustered. "Yes," Maria added, "A good size - for this room..." Frank seemed less than delighted by our comments, but agreed, nonetheless, how fortunate it was that it fit so well. Unfortunately, the rest of the decor fared even worse. It all had the feel of having been bought at the same store at the same time. The "art," for example, and photos were all print reproductions in typical store-bought frames: romantic scenes in Paris (he'd never been to Paris!), crashing into the sand (he hated the beach!). Frank was rushing too quickly into feeling established in a new home. But still, what could we say? The way he'd decorated wasn't going to help him move on with his life. It was just some catalog's life! He needed help.

For the rest of the evening, we gently supported him and maintained our "It's a good size" relative positivity. We had to be honest. We knew he'd find brighter days. As the months passed, we shopped with him occasionally. On his birthday, Maria gave him a painting which she'd done herself. It served as a springboard for a new interest Frank had never known before - original art. He eventually met a woman at a sculpting class, and the two, together, have developed a very rich, unique taste for fine art and home decor. ...And the rose-covered couch is long gone.

Mirrors are timeless, reflect light, open up a space to enlarge a room, reflect a window facing opposite to give another view of the outdoors, create positive energy, and showcase beauty as an affordable design element.

Barbara: "You can't have too many mirrors in a home. I have at least one in each room. In the kitchen I enjoy their equivalent - glass panels in some cabinet doors. Shiny, reflective surfaces always lift the spirits and make a room feel clean. The reflective nature of mirrors

Mirror, Mirror on the Wall

also simulates a lake, river or ocean, offering a calming influence."

Betty: "One large mirror or piece of art is preferred over many smaller items hanging on the wall. Mirrors come in different shapes. They repeat the room's design elements. Round mirrors can create interest over a chest of drawers. Oval or rectangular mirrors are generally used vertically as dressing mirrors in bathrooms and bedrooms. Horizontally, mirrors look great over a dining room buffet."

Repetition, Repetition, Repetition!

Repetition, Repetition, Repetition

Repetition in a room or entire home provides consistency, allows flow from one area to another, adds interest, and provides a cohesive, calming feeling. Repeating a paint color from room to room is especially important in a small house.

Stair spindles, with their vertical shapes, can be supported by stripes on the walls, wainscoting, or long, straight vertical mirrors, or pieces of art.

Repeat textures and colors. An extreme of this example is to design a room in monochromatic tones, like the entire room in different shades of white. Variations come in the form of textures in a fabric throw, decorative pillows, upholstered pieces of furniture, pictures, sculptures, books, lamps, carpet or area rugs, and window treatments.

This design principle can be used in landscape gardening as well. A scattering of various types and sizes of plantings can look chaotic. Group three or five of the same plant in an area for good composition. Repeat shades of green as well as colorful plants and flowers. An entire section of the same color flower looks better than several colors and varieties sharing the same small space. Look through garden catalogs or magazines for inspiration and award-winning combinations. Your local nursery is a good resource for suggesting plantings that are appropriate for your area.

Off THE WALL
Furniture
PLACEMENT

Off The Wall Furniture Placement

Barbara: "I don't know why most people think their furniture wants to hug the walls."

Practicality and visual interest increase when we float the furniture in the room. Even pulling the sofa a few inches from the wall is preferable.

It may seem like leaving a large open space in the center of the room will enlarge the room. The opposite is true. Removing extra pieces will enlarge the room, not pushing everything against the walls.

When people don't know where to put furniture it ends up on available wall space, between windows, doors, and the fireplace.

A furniture floor plan usually begins with where to put the TV. That positioning is usually established to accommodate electric and cable hookups, or to avoid glare from windows. Across from the TV usually resides the sofa, chairs, and recliner, all facing it from the opposing wall.

Betty: "Too much emphasis is put on the TV location. But then too much emphasis is put on watching TV."

Ideally a sitting area is formed in the center of the room to encourage conversation and interaction. Catalogs, magazines, TV shows, and movies showcase this design. You can still have furniture floating in the room and facing the TV.

Furniture placement should allow for traffic patterns to avoid bumping into furniture, end tables, or plants.

Beauty
with a
Brush
Latte
on the
Wall

Beauty with a Brush – Latte on the Wall

Paint colors have personalities. They evoke emotion. They can complement or contrast each other. They have temperatures, warm or cool. They have depth to go light or dark.

Color is not to be taken lightly. It can invigorate or calm. It can increase or suppress an appetite. It can make a room look large or small. It can make a ceiling appear high or low.

Fast food restaurants often use red and yellow. Red stimulates appetite, and both red and yellow excite. In a fast food restaurant those colors encourage people to eat and leave quickly. In restaurants that encourage a more relaxed experience, colors chosen are those found in nature and are calming: green, brown, beige, and blue.

Barbara's room color suggestions:

- KITCHEN – food colors; yellow, burgundy, green, etc. The colors should be muted, mixed with grey to establish a neutral hue. For example, green should be a grey/taupe green. Always consider how each color would look against the cabinets, countertops, trim, and floor.
- FAMILY ROOM – dark, deep colors enhance a room to be filled with activity, i.e., burgundy or chocolate.
- LIVING ROOM – beige, taupe, sage green, or grey-blue encourage relaxation.
- DINING ROOM – red or gold stimulate appetite and conversation.
- FOYER/HALLWAY – any neutral that is welcoming or a continuation of an adjacent room if the house is small.
- DEN or OFFICE – deep browns, beiges, taupes, or greens to enhance concentration and minimize distractions.
- LAUNDRY – bright, stimulating colors can be used here but most people opt for the green or blue family which is calming and neutral when in the grey tones.
- BATHROOM – browns, beiges, greens, and blues are often used as calming influences.
- BEDROOM – anything goes here but be aware that reds and oranges stimulate and may be inappropriate for kids' rooms.
- BASEMENT – white or soft, subtle colors are often used due to the lack of natural light from windows, but deep, rich tones create a more expensive, cozy feel.

Painting is a fast, inexpensive way to change the personality of a room. Mid to dark-toned colors give a room depth by absorbing light. They also make a room with a high ceiling feel cozier and less intimidating.

Ceiling paint choices are often not considered as most people buy flat white ceiling paint. This application is appropriate in many situations but bone white or very light beige is the best choice to coordinate with off-white trim and a deep, neutral wall color like grey-green. A white ceiling would look out of place in this instance. White is a cool color, and the surrounding colors are warm.

If a wall will be separated by a chair rail and each section will be painted a different color, the darker color should be chosen for the bottom. If an entire wall will be painted a different color, choose the focal wall to be the farthest from the entrance.

Paint selection can be a hazard for some people. One of Barbara's clients was a rabid sports fan and told her he wanted to paint the outside of his house his favorite team's colors. She quickly suggested he keep the colors neutral and consistent with the rest of the neighborhood. "When I told him how this may not sit well with his homeowners association, neighbors, passersby, and prospective buyers, he agreed with my suggestion to instead hang a flag or door banner on game day. Whew!"

Got
a
Light?

Got A Light?

Betty: "There are two types of lighting: ambient (overall) and task. Light from windows and overhead light combine to provide ambient lighting. Floor and table lamps are used for tasks like reading or sewing."

Barbara: "I like lots of light during the day but at night I light my life with candles or dimmer switches."

Bob: "If you ask me, I prefer darkness to light. Mice are nocturnal so we do much of our roaming in the dark. I can't comment on lighting since I'm just not that into it. I've repurposed matchsticks and a plastic condiment cup to make a lamp for my nightstand but it's strictly for aesthetics – no function whatsoever."

There are a few rules I adhere to with regard to lighting:

- Track lighting is for retail and theatre purposes only. It was never intended to be used in houses. Let's keep it that way.
- Chandeliers aren't for dining rooms only. They can make a dramatic statement in family rooms, living rooms, dens, libraries, and kitchens. I've even been in houses where they were used in closets. If you want drama, use a chandelier.
- Dimmer switches aren't for dining rooms only. Bathrooms are another application where less light is desired (middle of night and early morning), and more light is necessary (applying makeup, shaving). Bedrooms can also be considered for mood lighting with a dimmer switch.
- Lamps should be placed where needed for reading, using a computer, or sewing (task lighting), and overall lighting (ambient lighting) should be provided by a fixture on the ceiling. Built-in can lights (recessed lighting), flush-mount fixtures, or chandeliers are good choices.

A
WINDOW
to
the
WORLD

A Window To The World

Windows bring light into rooms while, at the same time, expanding the living space through their view to the outside.

Barbara: "Windows are great - the more the merrier. My rooms are bathed in windows. I keep my shades up all the time. It's like living in a fishbowl, but I don't mind. If people want to watch me live it's OK with me. It would be like watching a PG-13 movie I guess."

Betty: "There are many window treatment options but only two basics: shades and curtains/drapes/ scarves/valances. Functionally, you should be able to block out light or obtain privacy when desired. That's where the shades come in. Fashion comes when you choose the latter."

Maximize your outside view with a shade and valance (fabric or boxed) or a scarf. The valance or scarf will hide the shade when pulled up.

If you have curtains or drapes that close you can omit shades altogether. Mini-blinds can be manipulated to slant in various directions to control the amount of light and/or privacy and can be incorporated when curtains or drapes are kept open.

Scarves are usually sheer and used to frame a window with transparent, soft color. Shades are necessary with this option.

Valance options: fabric that is fed on a rod or made into a box. Shades are necessary.

Curtains (controlled on a pulley-style rod) add the versatility of insulation, texture, color, and sound absorption. Since they open and close easily, shades are optional.

Drapes (rod-fed or stationary on hooks/knobs) offer less insulation than fabric-backed curtains but do add texture, color, and sound absorption. Shades are optional if they can be closed but necessary if drapes are stationary on hooks or knobs.

There are many shade options: vertical, mini-blinds, two-inch wooden blinds, solid vinyl, or fabric to name a few.

Bob: "When I haven't had a manicure in a while, and my nails are long and sharp, I can scurry up curtains with ease. My upper-body strength and agility are incredible. I don't choose this route often but it comes in handy when being chased by a dog or cat."

I'm Floored!

I'm Floored

Barbara: "I live in high heels. They're great with gowns, dresses, skirts, and pants. They can, however, be a problem on hardwood floors."

Betty: "When choosing a flooring option, consider allergy sufferers. Carpeting, unless it is pure, untreated wool, will harbor allergens."

Hardwood floors can be used in all rooms indoors. They're durable, easy to clean, and a good choice for allergy sufferers. They can be refinished to change stain color or painted to create faux finishes. They are my floor of choice.

Marble is very porous. It stains easily, can be etched with spills like vinegar, and scratches easily. It can be installed edge-to-edge without grout.

Limestone can be an option if stone is desired, but it can be etched and is fragile. It can crack or break easily. This can be installed edge-to-edge without grout.

Ceramic tile is popular for its durability. It too can crack and break but is not susceptible to etching or staining. These tiles are usually installed with grout. Grout comes in a variety of colors. It can enhance your design options, but it is very porous and can stain easily.

Carpeting can be installed wall-to-wall or in carpet squares. A floating floor of carpet squares is an advantage when spills or pet accidents occur. The square can be removed, washed in the sink, dried, and returned, or, if the stain remains, replaced with another square. This is my choice for carpet options.

Pure wool carpeting is preferred for allergy sufferers but is easily stained since it is untreated and can only be dry cleaned.

Vinyl, also known as linoleum, is a popular choice for areas that are exposed to water (foyer, mudroom, laundry, kitchen, and bath). It is a "soft" floor that can tear and scratch.

Laminate floors by Pergo, Armstrong, Wilson Art, and Formica are hard, durable, easy to install, and are available in many styles and colors. They can show wear in heavy-traffic areas, can scratch, chip or peel, and are not recommended for wet areas.

BORAX
ARM & HAMMER
BAKING SODA

Part Four

Cleaning on a Diet

HOMEMADE, NATURAL CLEANERS!

CLEANING

Made FAST, CHEAP, & EASY

...with products you already own!

Cleaning Made Fast, Cheap, & Easy

A low-fat house will have an absolute minimum of cleaning supplies. The cleaning aisle in stores contains a myriad of specialty products. The sheer volume is overwhelming. Begin the process by replacing store-bought cleansers with homemade, natural cleansers. Retail household cleaning products contain ingredients that can be harmful to people, pets, and the environment. Fumes can be harmful to lungs and respiratory systems. Our skin absorbs harmful ingredients directly from touch or vapors. They become toxic and can accumulate over time. For example, a common grease-cutting ingredient found in over 200 common household products (2-butoxyethanol) has been identified by the EPA as having potential adverse effects on blood, central nervous system, kidneys, and liver. Other cleaning products contain chemicals like ammonia, phenol, chlorine, ethanol, cresol, and lye which can be dangerous and aren't necessary to keep your home clean and sparkling.

Betty will show you how to clean with what you already have in the kitchen or laundry, specifically baking soda, vinegar, vegetable oil, Borax, salt, lemon juice, club soda, and cream of tartar. They are natural and inexpensive.

Vinegar:

- Vinegar cuts grease, inhibits mold, mildew, bacteria, and kills germs. It's perfect for floors (except marble and limestone), windows, mirrors, toilets, and solid surfaces. It will shine chrome sink fixtures, and remove lime buildup. Vinegar can deodorize as well, removing odor from a room, microwave oven, or even clothing. It serves as a fabric softener when used in the rinse cycle of the wash and has the added benefit of keeping colors bright.
- Vinegar and baking soda together can declog a drain: ½ cup of each, cover drain, after 20 minutes flush with hot water.
- Vinegar can be used to clean and disinfect combs, brushes, remote controls, game controls, docking stations, cell phone, iPad, iPod, purse, backpack, computer bag, and/or briefcase. You can also make lights (bulbs and fixtures) sparkle by wiping with vinegar to make the whole room look cleaner and brighter.
- Vinegar can clean the coffee maker and dishwasher when run through a cycle followed by another cycle of water.
- Equal parts of vinegar and water will clear mineral deposits from an iron. Just fill, press steam button, turn off, let cool, and rinse.

- Vinegar can be used to remove carpet stains. Rub in, let sit a few minutes, blot dry.
- A natural air freshener can be made by combining 1 teaspoon baking soda, 1 teaspoon vinegar, and 2 cups hot water in a spray bottle. Spray in the air to remove odors.
- A natural furniture polish can be made with one teaspoon olive oil and ½ cup vinegar (you can also use lemon juice in place of vinegar for the lemony scent).
- Wet a cloth with vinegar and salt to clean copper. Add flour to the vinegar and salt mixture to clean brass.
- On clothing, rub vinegar into ketchup, blood, grass, fruit juice, and sweat stains, and let stand a few minutes before washing. Moldy towels benefit from soaking in vinegar for 10 to 20 minutes, then machine wash in hot water.
- To clean glass and mirrors mix equal parts vinegar and water in a pump spray bottle, spray on white lint-free cloth or paper towel. Do not spray directly onto mirror or glass as the drips can lodge behind the frame. Wipe clean with newspaper or coffee filter (does not leave newsprint ink).

Baking Soda:

Baking soda has so many uses I won't list them all here. I recommend the book by Arm & Hammer, "Pure Baking Soda For Baking, Cleaning & Deodorizing, Over 100 Helpful Household Hints."

White Flour:

Clean a toaster with kitchen flour! Rub with white flour on a dry rag to remove spots and provide a shine.

Borax:

- Borax is a water softener and sanitizer. It freshens laundry as well. When added to the wash it boosts the cleaning power of the laundry detergent so you can use half as much. It removes tough stains and is a natural alternative to color-safe bleach.
- Borax can be used on a porcelain or fiberglass tub since it cleans without scratching. It removes soap scum, hard water deposits, and dirt. It also eliminates odors.
- Borax and water will discourage mildew from forming and can be sprayed in the bath where needed.
- Borax can be used to clean the toilet. Sprinkle on, let stand 30 minutes or overnight, swish, and flush.
- Borax can be used to clean carpets and rugs: ½ cup dissolved in 1 pint water, sponged on, wait ½ hour, rinse, let dry, and vacuum.
- Borax can be used to clean counters and appliances when sprinkled on a damp sponge. It removes grease and can also be used to make dishes sparkling clean.

- Borax can clean the disposal and drain. Sprinkle 2-3 tablespoons, let stand 15 minutes, flush with water (disposal on).
- Borax can remove nail polish from a hard surface.
- Borax boosts the cleaning power of your dishwasher detergent by removing hard water minerals and residues. Add ¼ cup directly to bottom of dishwasher to reduce spots and film from dishes and glasses.
- Borax can be used to control insects. Sprinkle around outside foundation of house to keep them from entering your home.

Club Soda:

- Club soda applied immediately can remove most liquid stains from clothing or carpets.
- Dampen a cloth with club soda to clean a stainless steel sink, and buff with a dry cloth to shine.

Cream of Tartar:

- This can be used to remove stains from porcelain sinks, bathtubs, and from aluminum cookware.

Lemon Juice:

- Lemon juice can lighten stains, cut grease, and whiten whites. It is a mild bleaching agent so it is best used on white fabrics only. It can also be used to remove tarnish on brass, copper, bronze, and aluminum but do not use on silver.
- Lemon juice rubbed on your shower curtain will act as a natural disinfectant, dissolve soap scum and hard water deposits, while stopping mildew and eliminating odors.
- One tablespoon of lemon juice in a spray bottle with water will cut through grease and dirt to give windows a streak-free shine.
- To clean grout, add lemon juice to 1-2 teaspoons cream of tartar to make a paste, apply with a toothbrush and rinse.
- Use lemon juice to clean and rid your hands of fish, onion, or garlic smell from cooking.
- Lemon juice can bleach out stains (like tomato sauce residue) from plastic food containers. Rub lemon juice on stain, let dry in the sun, then wash as usual.

Salt:

- Salt can be used to absorb a red wine or coffee carpet spill. Let stand until all liquid is absorbed, then vacuum.
- Salt can also be sprinkled on a half lemon to clean a coffee maker pot, greasy pots and pans, and stained teacups and coffee mugs.

- When oven spills happen, sprinkle a heavy layer of salt to stop the smoking and odor, and continue cooking. Let the salt sit overnight, and lift the residue with a pancake turner or damp sponge.

Oil:

- Vegetable (or olive) oil can be used to polish furniture, chrome, season a wooden cutting board, and, when rubbed onto a stainless steel sink, will resist hard water stains.
- Olive oil wiped in a very thin layer over the shower door will deflect water and help stop mineral deposits. The glass will be easier to clean.
- Tea tree oil (2 teaspoons with 2 cups water shaken in a spray bottle) will destroy mold and mildew on contact. Use on walls, grout, tile, plastic shower liners, and shower curtains.

Betty's Cleaning Routine:

IN EACH ROOM: 1) use laundry basket to collect items that do not belong in room; 2) return items to their proper homes; 3) wipe down surfaces w/lemon oil cloth.

Then as follows:

Family Room: 4) vacuum drapes/chairs/ottoman/sofa/lampshades/baseboard/floor. Time 20:42. Cost: 1½ cents for ½ tsp. lemon oil on cloth.

Dining Room: 4) vacuum drapes/chairs/lampshades/baseboard/floor; 5) damp mop floor w/vinegar* or dish detergent. Time 8:51. Cost: 1½ cents for ½ tsp. lemon oil on cloth and 3 cents for 1 oz. vinegar or a few drops dish detergent on damp mop. Total cost 4½ cents.

Foyer: 4) vacuum drapes/floor/baseboards; 5) damp mop floor w/vinegar* or dish detergent. Time 4:02. Cost: 1½ cents for ½ tsp. lemon oil on cloth and 3 cents for 1 oz. vinegar or a few drops dish detergent on damp mop. Total cost 4½ cents.

*Do not use vinegar on marble or limestone floors.

Laundry Room: 4) vacuum drapes/floor/baseboards; 5) damp mop floor w/vinegar* or dish detergent. Time 4:05. Cost: 1½ cents for ½ tsp. lemon oil on cloth and 3 cents for 1 oz. vinegar or a few drops dish detergent on damp mop. Total cost 4½ cents.

Kitchen: Sprinkle ¼ cup baking soda in wet sink, scrub, and let sit until kitchen is done; 4) wipe counters/stovetop/appliances/cabinets/inside microwave w/dish detergent; 5) use club soda on cloth to clean and shine stainless steel appliances; 6) vacuum drapes/floor/baseboards; 7) damp mop floor w/ vinegar* or dish detergent; 8) scrub and rinse baking soda from sink. Time 21:46. Cost: 2 cents for 1 oz. club soda, 3 cents for a few drops of dish detergent on damp cloth and 3 cents for 3 tsp. baking soda. Total cost 8 cents.

Office/Den: 4) vacuum drapes/chairs/lampshades/baseboard/floor; 5) damp mop floor w/vinegar* or dish detergent. Time 4:27. Cost: 1½ cents for ½ tsp. lemon oil on cloth and 3 cents for 1 oz. vinegar or a few drops dish detergent on damp mop. Total cost 4½ cents.

Back Entrance/Mud Room: 4) vacuum drapes/baseboard/floor; 5) damp mop floor w/vinegar* or dish detergent. Time 2:56. Cost: 1½ cents for ½ tsp. lemon oil on cloth and 3 cents for 1 oz. vinegar or a few drops dish detergent on damp mop. Total cost 4½ cents.

Powder Room (Half Bath): Sprinkle baking soda in toilet bowl and sink, scrub, and let sit until room is done; 4) wipe mirror with coffee filter; 5) vacuum drapes/floor/baseboards; 6) damp mop floor w/ vinegar* or dish detergent; 7) scrub and rinse baking soda from toilet bowl and sink. Time 4:11. Cost: 1½ cents for ½ tsp. lemon oil on cloth, 3 cents for 1 oz. vinegar or a few drops dish detergent on damp mop, and 4 cents for 4 tsp. baking soda. Total cost 8½ cents.

Bathroom: Heat one cup (8 oz.) white vinegar. 4) moisten cloth w/warm vinegar to clean mirror; 5) dry mirror with coffee filter; 6) wipe shower enclosure and tub with warm vinegar on cloth, and dry w/towel; 7) follow above routine for half bath. Time 7:35. Cost: 1½ cents for ½ tsp. lemon oil on cloth, 24 cents for 8 oz. vinegar, and 4 cents for 4 tsp. baking soda. Total cost 29½ cents.

Bedroom: 4) make bed; 5) vacuum drapes/lampshades/baseboard/floor. Time 6:45. Cost: 1½ cents for ½ tsp. lemon oil on cloth.

Tip: For the budget-conscious, you can reuse the lemon oil cloth to dust more than one room - a savings of 1½ cents per room.

*Do not use vinegar on marble or limestone floors.

Part Five

The Results at a Glance

Before & After

PHOTOS

Loss of Pounds

and Inches

The Cluttered Family Room — *Pounds & Inches*

1. Desk/chair/secretary/floor lamp ----------------119 lbs., 57,462"
2. Dog bed/dog toys ------------------------------------ 7 lbs., 5,220"
3. Top of 2 tables/coffee table ----------------------- 83 lbs., 13,245"
4. Magazine table/ball/shoes ------------------------- 53 lbs., 9,259"
5. Laundry basket/table ------------------------------ 59 lbs., 17,159"
6. Clothes/hall tree ------------------------------------ 5 lbs., 1,686"
7. Fireplace items mantle/hearth ------------------- 51 lbs., 13,268"
8. Sofa items -- 5 lbs., 5,580"

Here's what we did:
Pounds & Inches Lost = 382 lbs., 122,879"

Recycled newspapers/magazines, donated extra florals, created storage for toys/books, put away clothes, moved furniture to son's condo.

The Cluttered Kitchen — *Pounds & Inches*

1. Desktop items -- 12 lbs., 2,376”
2. Left counter items -----------------------------------37 lbs., 5,045”
3. Fridge -- 0 lbs., 584”
4. Island items --- 13 lbs., 1,807”
5. Top of cabinets --------------------------------------- 5 lbs., 20,736”
6. Right counter items ------------------------------- 37 lbs., 8,660”
7. Forward counter items ---------------------------------- 1 lbs., 161”
8. Right of sink counter items ------------------------ 12 lbs., 2,120”

Here's what we did:
Pounds & Inches Lost = 117 lbs., 41,489"

Sold baskets, donated extras in cabinets to create storage for counter items, filed refrigerator front papers.

The Cluttered Pantry — *Pounds & Inches*

1. Pet taxi --- 9 lbs., 2,299"
2. Wall items --- 2 lbs., 3,870"
3. Front of cabinets -- 0 lbs., 508"
4. Countertop items ---------------------------------- 45 lbs., 14,466"

Here's what we did:
Pounds & Inches Lost = 56 lbs., 21,143"

Moved pet taxi to garage, boxed best of kids artwork, discarded the rest, donated extras in cabinets to create storage for counter items.

The Cluttered Dining Room *Pounds & Inches*

1. Items on buffet ------------------------------------ 171 lbs., 19,362”
2. Floor lamp -- 22 lbs., 25,704”
3. Left side chair with toys ---------------------------- 39 lbs., 37,816”
4. Table and 4 chairs ------------------------------ 330 lbs., 122,646”
5. Items on table top -------------------------------- 76.5 lbs., 12,452”
6. Plant on top of stand/mantle items ------------ 21.5 lbs., 79,689”
7. Items on floor -- 26 lbs., 4,644”
8. Side chair w/coats and stuffed animals --------- 42 lbs., 48,272”

Here's what we did:
Pounds & Inches Lost = 728 lbs., 350,585"

Sold buffet/mantle items, donated toys/games, moved large plant/ floor lamps/table/chairs to son's condo, recycled papers, stored wrapping/sewing/craft items in basement cabinet.

The Cluttered Florida Room — *Pounds & Inches*

1. Baskets -- 21 lbs., 10,060”
2. Table clutter -- 6 lbs., 1,358”
3. Shoes -- 2 lbs., 720”
4. Floor plants -------------------------------------- 13 lbs., 34,056”
5. Table/chairs --------------------------------------- 51 lbs., 46,800”
6. Ottoman clutter ------------------------------------- 4 lbs., 432”
7. Bookbags/basket of blankets -------------------- 46 lbs., 11,709”
8. Balls --- 1 lbs., 1,233”

Here's what we did:
Pounds & Inches Lost = 144 lbs., 106,368"

Gave away games/ottoman/2 plants, sold table/chairs, and returned book bags/blankets/reading material/shoes to their permanent homes.

The Cluttered Laundry Room *Pounds & Inches*

1. Top of washer/dryer (towels/black bag) ------------20 lbs., 4,080"
2. Counter items (left basket/buckets/ right 2 watering cans – both counters) ------------ 9.5 lbs., 9,171"
3. Window items -- 1 lbs., 54"
4. Hanging clothes -- 6 lbs., 900"
5. Ironing board/iron -------------------------------- 20 lbs., 10,637"
6. Basket -- 12 lbs., 3,179"
7. Bags/hanging mops --------------------------------- 4 lbs., 6,375"
8. Right counter items -------------------------------- 13 lbs., 1,384"

Here's what we did:
Pounds & Inches Lost = 85.5 lbs., 35,780"

Stored mops/bags/watering cans in garage, donated extra tubs/pots/cabinet items to create more storage, put away laundry and ironing board/iron.

The Cluttered Office	Pounds & Inches
1. Left side desktop items	42 lbs., 2,211"
2. Top shelf items	58 lbs., 7,200"
3. Right side desktop	68 lbs., 6,344"
4. Trash can	18 lbs., 2,016"
5. Corner desktop items	32 lbs., 9,384"
6. Below corner desk	26 lbs., 3,342"
7. Right front of corner desk items	20 lbs., 2,632"
8. Stack	10 lbs., 2,223"

Here's what we did:
Pounds & Inches Lost = 274 lbs., 35,352"

Purged files, recycled papers/phone books, donated extra books/ photo albums/binders, discarded unnecessary items in drawers to create more storage.

The Cluttered Library | **Pounds & Inches**

1. Left section --- 72 lbs., 3,250”
2. Middle section ------------------------------------- 111 lbs., 5,169”
3. Right section --94 lbs., 3,951”
4. Corner section--- 25 lbs., 1,232”
5. Desk chair -- 7 lbs., 4,074”
6. Desktop items -- 18 lbs., 1,090”
7. Desk -- 33 lbs., 9,632”

Here's what we did:
Pounds & Inches Lost = 360 lbs., 28,398"

Donated books, recycled magazines/catalogs, sold desk/chair, rearranged books and decorative items.

The Cluttered Bathroom	*Pounds & Inches*
1. Grooming supplies	12 lbs., 1,270"
2. Towels and toothpaste	5.5 lbs., 1,572"
3. Top shelf	6 lbs., 480"
4. Middle shelf	7 lbs., 912"
5. Bottom shelf	2 lbs., 376"
6. Trash can	2 lbs., 500"
7. Dirty laundry	4.5 lbs., 2,312"
8. Cleaning supplies	2 lbs., 945"

Here's what we did:
Pounds & Inches Lost = 41 lbs., 8,367"

Eliminated cleaning supplies, cleared unnecessary items from cabinets, put away countertop and shelf items, removed laundry.

The Cluttered Guest Room — *Pounds & Inches*

1. Items on and under desk ---------------------------- 31 lbs., 2,835"
2. Floor items by ironing board ---------------------- 37 lbs., 17,262"
3. Ironing board/iron ---------------------------------- 7 lbs., 29,950"
4. Left of dresser ------------------------------------ 40 lbs., 10,458"
5. Right of dresser ------------------------------------ 76 lbs., 49,104"
6. Crib and contents ---------------------------------- 16 lbs., 62,424"
7. On and right of daybed ---------------------------- 36 lbs., 14,364"
8. Vacuum cleaner ------------------------------------ 15 lbs., 12,096"

Here's what we did:
Pounds & Inches Lost = 258 lbs., 198,493"

Donated crib/bedding/pillows/extra luggage, recycled tubs of kids old school papers, made room in closet for ironing board, craft/sewing items, and vacuum.

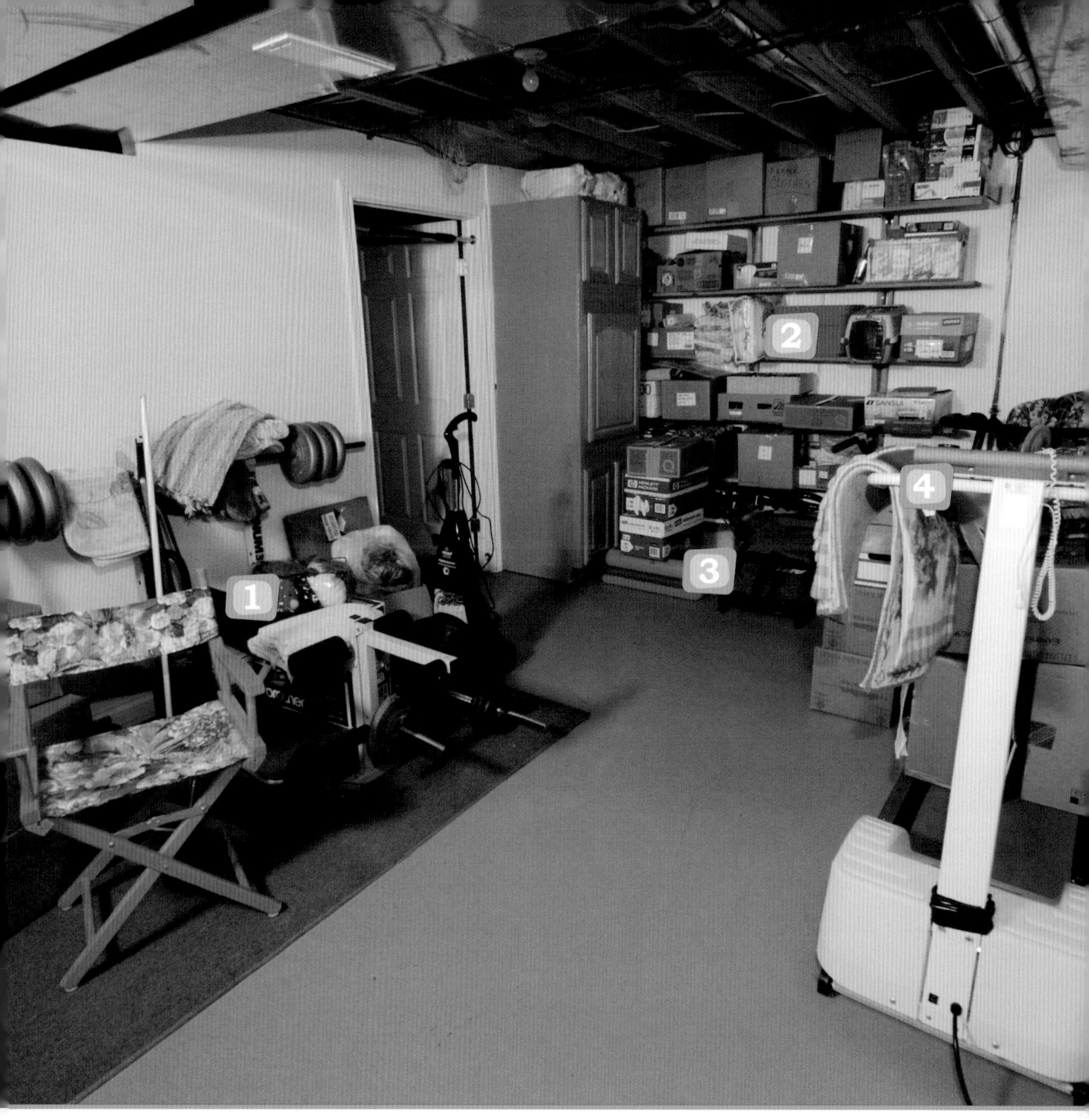

The Cluttered Exercise Room — *Pounds & Inches*

1. Left equipment area ------------------------------ 113 lbs., 66,936"
2. Shelving -- 312 lbs., 68,040"
3. Floor items (front of shelves) ---------------------- 58 lbs., 18,240"
4. Right items in/on equipment -------------------- 136 lbs., 41,232"

Here's what we did:
Pounds & Inches Lost = 619 lbs., 194,448"

Donated extra area rugs, cat carrier, clothes, dishes, glassware, and decorations from shelf boxes. Sold chair and carpet cleaner.

The Cluttered Basement **Pounds & Inches**

1. 1st row – left wall shelves ------------------------ 192 lbs., 40,656”
2. Hanging wreaths & décor --------------------------- 3 lbs., 5,670”
3. Left wall bookcase ---------------------------------- 13 lbs., 3,696”
4. Left floor items ----------------------------------- 378 lbs., 158,776”
5. Center floor items ------------------------------ 228 lbs., 109,328”
6. Right floor items/bookshelf -------------------- 391 lbs., 164,548”
7. Tabletop items ------------------------------------ 70 lbs., 35,670”

Here's what we did:
Pounds & Inches Lost = 1,275 lbs., 518,344"

Recycled papers, sold and/or donated decorative and craft items.

The Cluttered Garage	Pounds & Inches
1. Front items	114.5 lbs., 10,661”
2. Left items	48 lbs., 10,782”
3. 4 bins	52 lbs., 22,032”
4. 7 bins/wreath/Santa picture	137 lbs., 19,303”
5. Center stacked items	411 lbs., 56,588”
6. Above cabinet items	120 lbs., 51,567”

Here's what we did:
Pounds & Inches Lost = 882.5 lbs., 170,933"

Sold cooler/tub/bench/swing/power washer/card table/chairs and decorative items. Donated two Christmas trees/ornaments/stand and two canopy tents.

Part Six

Recipes for Low-Fat Rooms

Recipes for
LOW-FAT
ROOMS

Recipes For Low-Fat Rooms

The ingredients in these recipes are the absolute minimum required for the designated activity to take place. Remember, we're putting each room on a diet. We're trying to get rid of unnecessary weight, lighten the load, and reduce clutter. While it seems like common sense, we still need to be reminded of the purpose and activity dedicated to each room of the house.

It's hard for some people to be objective and to decide to let things go. If you evaluate the usefulness of each item in the room, you stand a better chance for success. Each recipe's instructions begin with "remove everything from the room." This step is not an option. Only when everything is out of the room can you objectively evaluate the space, the focal point, and the room's purpose. Looking at the empty room is the only way to look at it with an open mind. It empowers you to determine what goes back in, needs to be recycled, or can be given to someone else to enjoy.

Each room can lose a significant amount of pounds and inches as evidenced in "The Result at a Glance" section of before and after photos. It's amazing to see how much weight and inches you can lose by discarding, donating, or recycling. This diet really works. You will be pleased with the results.

House dieting should become a lifestyle – a healthy habit. As a result you:

- Become aware of clutter.
- Feel good about giving items away when you don't need them anymore.
- Become a savvy shopper, reluctant to bring clutter into your home.

We've heard stories or known people who have lost weight and kept it off. It can happen when you put your house on a diet too. Your house will keep the weight off if you remain diligent in purging on a regular basis and questioning new purchases.

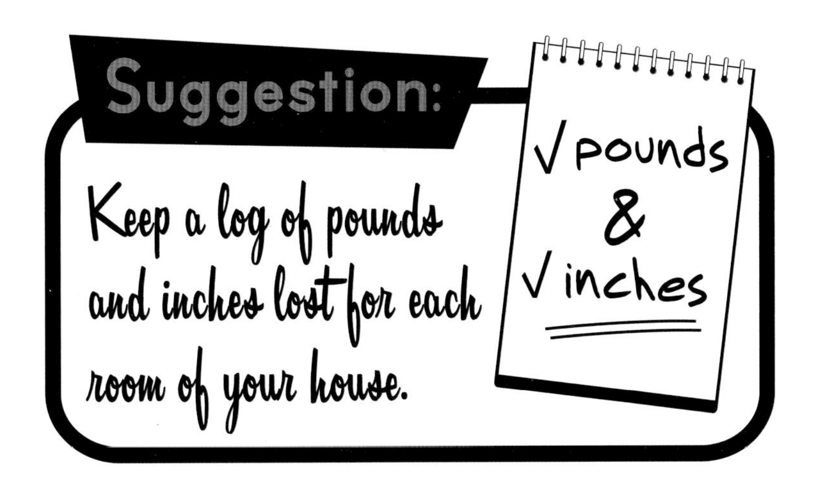

Recipe for a LOW-FAT FOYER

Ingredients
✓ clean closet
✓ hangers for guests
✓ mirror or art
✓ door mat
✓ seating (optional)

1. Take everything out of the room and closet.
2. Determine storage, furniture, mirror/art, and lighting needs.
3. Paint, wash, or enjoy walls.
4. Replace or clean floor.
5. Install hooks, mirror/art, lighting.
6. Reintroduce fabulous, functional, foyer finds.

A thoughtful hostess empties the closet ahead of time...

...and provides enough hangers for all guests to hang their coats in the closet. This shows respect for their belongings and makes it fast and easy to retrieve them when leaving.

I always love a mirror!

Mirrors have been foyer staples for as long as I can remember. They are useful when putting on hats, scarves, coats, or getting one last look before leaving. They also provide a warm welcome when arriving.

*F*irst impressions are very important. When someone comes to the front door, this may be the only room they see. When guests arrive, this is their welcome.

Betty: "This room should say 'hello,' not 'look at our shoes, mail, book bags, purse, briefcase, toys, laundry to go upstairs, etc.' This room is your greeter. It needs to be clear of daily chores and visible storage."

The foyer closet is intended for guests to put their coats, hats, or umbrellas. Unfortunately, we fill this space with games, camera equipment, vacuum cleaner and accessories, American flag, leaves from the dining room table, shoes, every jacket and coat we own, boots, hats, mittens, scarves, items to return to the store, bags with donations, light bulbs, and other household sundries.

There's certainly very little or no room for guests. When they arrive in the winter, their coats get piled on a sofa, or a chair, or are taken to the master bedroom. When someone leaves, they have to dig through the pile to find their coat.

Door mats are functional for catching dirt and moisture from shoes. They prevent dirt from being tracked in from outside.

Betty: "I encourage everyone to remove their shoes. They not only track in dust, dirt, snow, salt, etc., but they can also carry in imbedded stones that can scratch hardwood floors. Wearing slippers or walking barefoot also keeps the sound level down, and everyone appreciates that."

Barbara: "I remember working with a client in her basement office and hearing family members upstairs walking on the hardwood floors with shoes. It sounded like a herd of elephants."

One final item for the low-fat foyer that is optional is seating. A chair or bench is useful for sitting down to remove/put on shoes and/or boots.

"I don't use the foyer much as we mice don't enter and exit a house through doors. It's too visible to the rest of the house (and all its occupants), so I usually visit this room at night. Since there's no food or water, and it's a wide-open, boring space, I usually just pass through when running to other rooms."

1. Take everything out of the room.
2. Evaluate storage needs.
3. Paint, wash, or enjoy walls.
4. Replace or clean floor, toilet, tub/shower, shower curtain/liner, sink, faucets.
5. Install hooks/towel bar and storage (cabinet/basket/shelves).
6. Incorporate mirror, art, and accessories.

Notice I didn't add toilet brush or plunger to the list of ingredients?

While these items are necessary to have on hand, they don't need to be sitting on the floor next to the toilet for everyone to see. If you have a vanity sink cabinet, I suggest using it for storing these and the waste basket - out of sight, out of mind.

The powder room can be stylish!

People think that since the room is small they need small prints on the wall. That's not the case. A few large prints are the right scale for this room to give warmth, color, personality, and a sense of style. I suggest bold, dark colors for the walls and large scale art or mirrors.

To keep things simple and easy to clean:

1. Omit throw rugs: they make the room look smaller and cleaning the floor becomes a two-step process.
2. Omit the magazine rack. It's hard to clean around and collects dust.
3. Keep the toilet tank top clear.
4. Omit above-the-toilet units that encourage clutter.
5. Keep nothing but soap on the pedestal sink or vanity. You can also include a folded towel if you don't have a towel holder on the wall.

Clutter can also hide in the vanity sink cabinet. A low-fat room would only house the toilet brush, plunger, cleaning supplies, extra toilet paper, air freshener spray, extra towels, and waste basket. The exception: family members using this room regularly to get ready. Personal grooming supplies should be kept together in a plastic tub or basket.

Ideally, lighting should be adjustable (dimmer switch). Sometimes you want bright light (putting on makeup or getting something out of your eye), and sometimes you don't.

Barbara: "I remember a client who took some of the light bulbs out of her fixture because she said it was too bright first thing in the morning. It looked like deferred maintenance all the time - like she kept forgetting to buy new light bulbs. I suggested she replace all the empty sockets with new bulbs and install a dimmer switch."

"I think it's disgusting when a dog or cat drinks out of the toilet bowl. How uncouth, not to mention unsanitary. I prefer a dripping faucet or leaky pipe. At least I know the water is clean. Other than coming here for a quick drink or sponge bath, I steer clear - too many toxic cleaning supplies. I don't even want to think about the germs festering on the toilet brush and plunger! Ugh, get me out of here!"

Recipe for a LOW-FAT FAMILY ROOM

Ingredients
✓ comfortable seating
✓ adequate lighting
✓ table(s)
✓ TV (optional)
✓ window treatments
✓ accessories

1. Take everything out of the room.
2. Identify focal point: Fireplace or TV? It could be both.
3. Evaluate wall color, window treatments, lighting, accessories, art, and furniture needs.
4. Wash, paint, or enjoy your walls.
5. Replace or clean flooring.
6. Replace furniture and accessories sparingly, highlighting your focal point.
7. Plan a cocktail party for intimate friends.

Ask yourself: What is your family room used for?

Relaxing, entertaining, watching TV, using the computer, playing the piano, playing games?

How many adults live in your home?

There's usually only one person watching TV or reading in the family room most of the time. Even when others join in to watch TV or play a game, you can get by with one sofa and a few chairs. I've observed that young kids sit on the floor for both activities. How many adults live in the home? That's what you should look at when paring down the seating for everyday living.

When you take everything out of the room, you will have a clean perspective on the most efficient use of space, and you'll notice the walls, windows, and floor more. Are you happy with the wall color?

Window treatments should be functional and fabulous. You can get by with only valances or window scarves if you have shades to pull down for privacy or to block the sun. Otherwise, you'll need drapes that close. Hang rods close to the ceiling - yes, above the window frame by several inches. This makes the room look taller and provides drama around the windows. If you don't believe me, look in design/home magazines.

Position the sofa at an angle to face the fireplace or TV. Then place your chairs. The coffee table should be in front of the sofa. End tables can flank the sofa or chair(s) to rest the remote control(s), reading material, lamp, etc.

Try not to block windows and doors. It's not only OK to place furniture floating in the center of the room, but preferred. Don't make the mistake that furniture has to hug the walls. Designers for movies, TV shows, catalogs, and magazines place furniture in the center of the room, and you should as well. Additional furniture may be needed for storage and/or specific activities like a computer desk or piano. These items can, and probably should, hug the walls.

Add accessories. Pictures or mirrors should be big in scale. Decorative objects, including plants, should be sparse. That way they'll get lots of attention.

Lamps should be placed where needed for reading or using a computer (task lighting). Overall lighting (ambient lighting) should be provided by a fixture on the ceiling or floor lamps.

"Family rooms are great. There's usually crumbs, books, toys, games, magazines, newspapers, etc., lots of stuff to nibble at, collect, and repurpose with plenty of room to roam. I do my fast-walking, running, and ab crunches here. I will hang around to watch TV only if an old film noir movie is on - not worth getting spotted otherwise. My favorite pastime is stealing a puzzle piece - just one, mind you. It makes for great art on the wall in my living space. The most fun is listening to Homeowner blame everyone for losing it and ruining the whole puzzle. It's the only cruel thing I do."

Recipe for a LOW-FAT LIVING ROOM

Ingredients
- ✓ comfortable seating
- ✓ adequate lighting
- ✓ table(s)
- ✓ window treatments
- ✓ accessories

1. Take everything out of the room.
2. Determine focal point.
3. Paint, wash, or enjoy walls.
4. Replace or clean floor.
5. Evaluate furniture, art, and accessories.
6. Reincorporate the minimum of above.
7. Savor your retreat.

It's not a museum!

If you use this room for entertaining, reading, doing homework, or just plain relaxing on occasion, that's great. Remember the example I gave for how much you spend in taxes for seldom-used rooms? If the living room is 6-10 percent of your home's square feet, you're spending several hundred dollars a year just to have that extra space. Don't put your most expensive furniture and accessories in there unless you're charging admission and offering a tour. You still have to dust and vacuum, so you might as well enjoy the space as often as possible.

Plastic is for credit cards, not furniture.

I remember visiting Mary and sneaking into the 'forbidden room' just to see what it was like to sit on a plastic-covered sofa. If you sat on it for too long, it made an indentation that we frantically tried to get out before being caught.

*H*omes with both family rooms and living rooms usually reserve the living room for "company." This room is often furnished with more expensive, formal furniture and is rarely used.

Expensive, formal seating is not always synonymous with comfort. It doesn't even look welcoming. You can soften the look with accent pillows or a throw. One sofa and a loveseat or a chair or two is sufficient.

Betty: "Cabinets can be used for storage, but be careful not to collect clutter here."

Coffee table and end tables should offer a place to put drinks or a book. Lamps can be placed on end tables. Floor lamps are often necessary, as many living rooms are built without overhead lighting.

Windows will need shades or drapes for privacy and to block the sun's harmful UV rays, which can damage expensive fabrics.

Accessories should be kept to a minimum. What you do display will receive prominence and be more appreciated.

Art should be large in scale. Mirrors can open up space and showcase the outdoors when positioned to reflect a window. See "Mirror, Mirror on the Wall."

Pianos are often found in this room if they aren't housed in the family room. A baby grand piano takes up lots of space and leaves very little for seating. Barbara has been in more than one home where there was a baby grand in the living room. She recalls, "Janice had just the piano and art on the wall. Another client had a harp and a grand piano, but she did play for the Symphony and used both on a daily basis."

Sometimes the living room is used as an office. See "Recipe for a Low-Fat Office" for ingredients and suggestions.

"I have to admit, the most boring room in a house, for a mouse, is the living room - no food or water. Who would want to take up shelter in such a stuffy atmosphere? Not me. The only fun here is running through the piano innards. I have to be very careful not to step on a chord or I'll blow my cover - be found out - and it could cost me my life. Needless to say, I don't spend much time here."

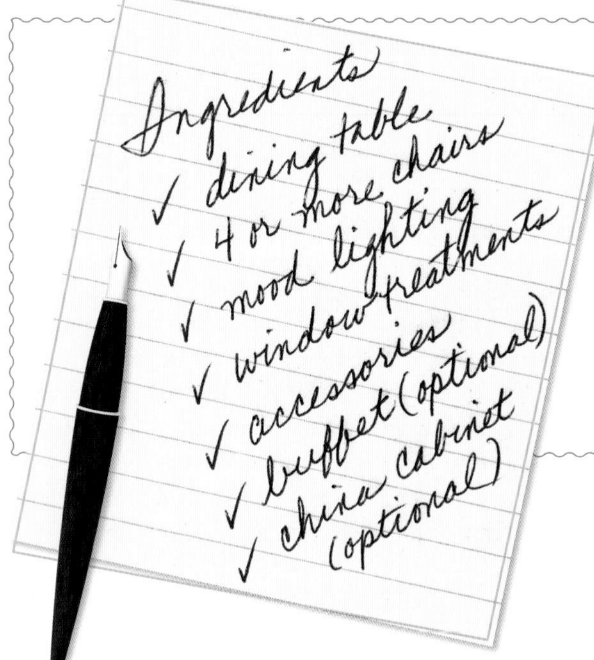

1. Take everything out of the room.
2. Evaluate lighting, window treatments, storage, and seating.
3. Paint, wash, or enjoy walls.
4. Replace or clean floor.
5. Reincorporate furniture necessary for daily living/storage.
6. Add art, mirror, and accessories.
7. Enjoy dining in a relaxing atmosphere with family/friends.

Make your dining room worth its weight!

Let's say you have a 2,000 square foot home and your taxes are $8,000 per year. The dining room is 10 x 12 (120 square feet). This room takes up 6 percent of your home so the tax you are paying on that room alone is $480 a year. If you eat in the dining room only on Thanksgiving, Christmas, and Easter, each meal costs $160, and that's not including food, drinks, tablecloth, and seasonal décor.

I'm big on dinner parties and hosting family celebrations!

Dining rooms are formal eating rooms, not catchalls for miscellaneous items.

*Y*ou don't have to have a formal dining room set to enjoy this room every day. On a budget? Put a white sheet over a folding table. It will drape enough to cover the legs. Want to be creative? Use a pedestal plant stand (or two for a larger table) and add a salvaged table top. Folding chairs have come a long way and are now made with wood frames and upholstered seats. Extras store nicely so you can have seating on hand for entertaining, or you can purchase second-hand chairs. They don't have to match. Paint them the same color to look like a set.

The wall color you choose should reflect the mood of a dining experience - typically red, gold, green, or blue.

Accessorize with wall art, a mirror over the buffet, a table centerpiece, and one large item on the buffet.

Lighting should be flexible to create a dining atmosphere (dimmer switch). Recessed lights built into the ceiling or a chandelier hung over the table work best.

Window shades or drapes complete the room and are necessary to block the sun when dining.

Minimum furniture for a dining room would be a table and chairs. Formal dining room sets include a buffet for storage and serving, and a china cabinet for storage. Some dining rooms collect unwanted furniture from other areas of the house, like grandma's old sewing cabinet. If no one in the family sews, get rid of it. For sentimentality purposes, take a picture for the photo album, and donate it. The exception would be if you are using it as a buffet for serving.

When toys, crafts, projects, games, paperwork, newspapers, unread mail, etc., cover the tabletop, there's no room to dine. Assign permanent homes in appropriate areas for non-dining items, deleting, of course, that which is no longer used, needed, or loved.

Bottom line: if you have a dining room, clear it out for dining with family and friends!

> "Other than searching for crumbs, I don't spend much time here unless someone is doing crafts or wrapping presents. I like to chew off a small piece of wrapping paper, frame it with matchsticks, and hang it on the wall for instant art."

Recipe for a LOW-FAT KITCHEN

1. Empty cabinets and counters.
2. Ruthlessly go through fridge.
3. Paint, wash, or enjoy walls.
4. Replace or clean floor.
5. Wipe cabinets inside and out (liner optional).
6. Eliminate duplicates, decide on donations.
7. Store most countertop items in cabinets.
8. Savor your counter space expanse.

Find everything a home.

Storing as many objects in cabinets and off the counters as possible keeps the kitchen clean and provides maximum counter space.

You just can't keep guests out of the kitchen.

When I have people over, they always hang out in the kitchen with me. Since I keep my counters clear at all times, there's plenty of space for a party bar, appetizers, and fresh flowers from a suitor.

"When the kitchen is clean, my whole house feels clean!" says one of Barbara's clients.

The kitchen is the hub of a home and is the family's most utilized room. Unfortunately, it often becomes the dumping ground for purses, papers, book bags, shopping purchases, food, and dirty dishes.

Many kitchen gadgets are available, but the basics can usually do the job. Only add what you will use regularly and can't live without.

Betty: "Find homes for your canisters, toaster, mixer, and other small appliances. A coffee maker can be left out, but toasters are so unappealing (especially toaster ovens that are hard to clean). They should be kept in a lower cabinet. Knife blocks take up valuable countertop space and should also be stored.

When I stage a house to sell, I only allow the coffee maker and decorative objects on the counters. Everything else looks like clutter and reminds prospective buyers of work, especially paper products like paper towels and napkins. I also advocate a 'naked' sink and refrigerator. Store the dish drainer, soaps, sponge, etc., under the sink for showings. Take everything off the refrigerator – top, front, and sides. When a house is clean and clutter-free, it sells quickly."

It's common to have duplicate kitchen gadgets. Taking everything out of the kitchen forces you to examine the inventory. You'll find things you haven't seen in a long time. Donate items you haven't used or know you will never use. Donate your duplicates. Discard anything broken.

When you are ready to put useful items away, determine the location where you use each item most. Adhere to the rule of keeping like things together and assigning a permanent home in the most convenient location.

"Most mice spend a lot of time in the kitchen, and I'm no exception. We have three basic needs: food, shelter, and water. The kitchen provides all three. Plus it's usually where the junk drawer is located, and I LOVE junk drawers! There are so many great things to repurpose for my living space. I mentioned most of them in my introduction letter at the beginning of this book so I won't bore you here with details."

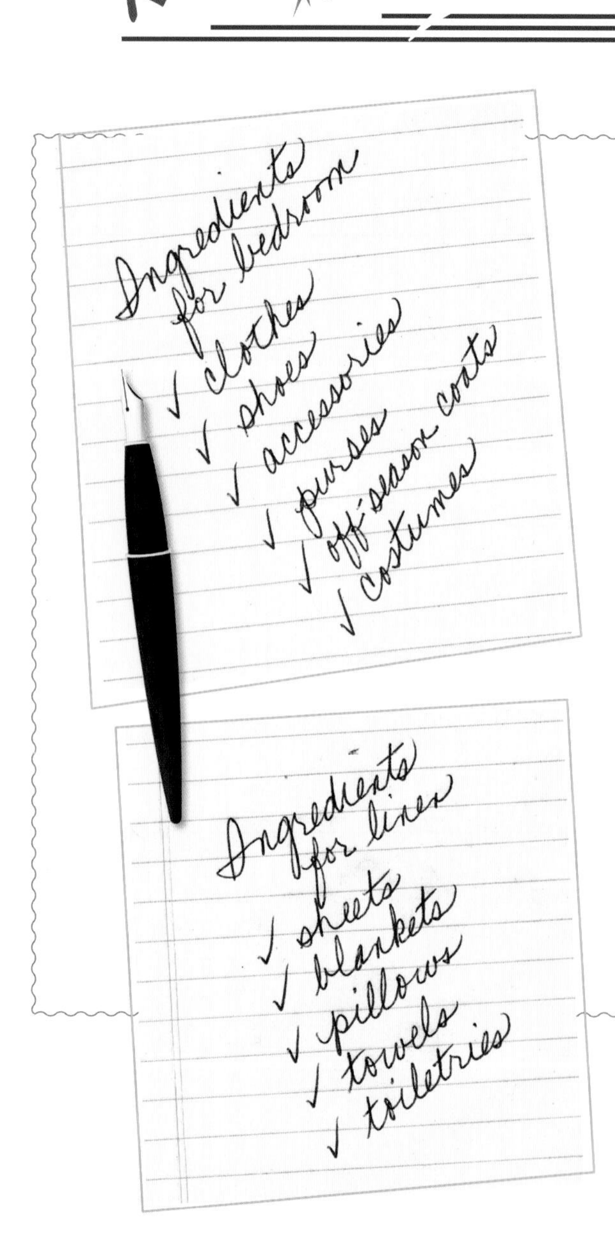

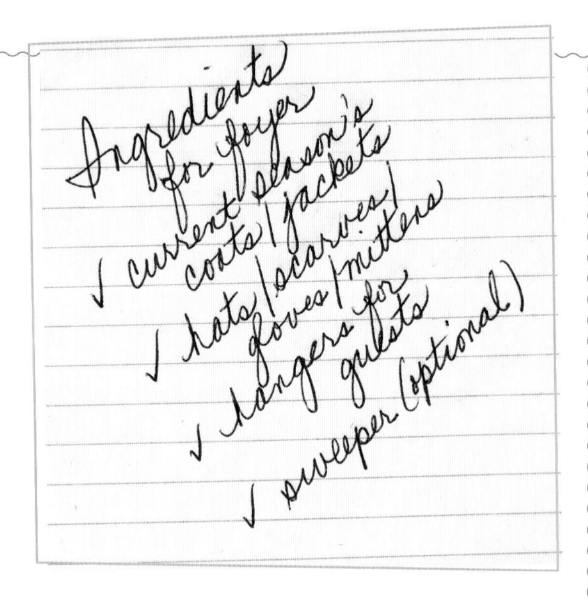

1. Take everything out of the closet.
2. Paint, wash, or enjoy walls.
3. Fill donation bags.
4. Replace loved items that still look great.
5. Savor the extra space.

Keep it in season!

Take everything out of the closet to decide on the most appropriate home. When only seasonal jackets/coats are hung, it provides room for guests or just more breathing space for you.

One must make room for new clothes.

I regularly purge my closets to make room for new gowns.

Barbara and Betty have never met a closet that didn't need to go on a diet. Regular purging and organizing is ideal to know what you own and where to find it.

Many of Barbara's clients keep their vacuum cleaner in this closet for convenience. This is the only item that should be stored on the floor of a low-fat foyer closet. Hats, scarves, and mittens can be stored in a bin on the shelf.

Betty: "I had a client that was a clean freak and told me she rotated closet cleaning every month. She took everything out, wiped down the walls and shelf, swept the floor, and only put back items she needed. According to her, she used to buy duplicates all the time, and this was her solution to knowing exactly what she had on hand."

"Closets make great homes for mice. They are so jam-packed with stuff that there's always great hiding potential. We like to feel safe and secure, and closets are a great place where people don't hang out. It's usually quiet and serene. It's where I go to meditate and do Yoga."

1. Take everything out of the pantry.
2. Paint, wash, or enjoy walls/shelves.
3. Eliminate duplicates and never-used items.
4. Fill donation bag/box.
5. Replace cherished and useful items.
6. Enhance organization with bins/baskets for like items.
7. Enjoy everything at a glance.

Let go of the overflow!

Pantries tend to become catchalls for kitchen item overflow. A diet is necessary to get rid of never-used items.

If you can't have a butler, at least have a butler's pantry!

I just love friends who have planned a butler's pantry in their home when entertaining is their focus. For me, it's all about getting together with friends and enjoying drinks and good food.

Originally, a butler's pantry was used as a staging area for the butler to place food on trays to carry to the dining table. In homes today, it's still designed as a pass-through area off the kitchen.

Barbara: "Ideally, one would hire a five-star butler who would never allow clutter - some scientifically engineered Jeeves who is genetically predisposed to despise messiness and disorganization.".

It's a luxury to have a butler's pantry off the kitchen or dining room. They're great to store serving pieces for entertaining. Unfortunately, it provides another area to accumulate more rarely-used items.

Betty: "Several clients I've worked with use the butler's pantry to store wine glasses and bottles of wine as well as service platters for appetizers. Others outfit a full bar with liquor and mixers."

The kitchen pantry can store food, paper products, small appliances, spices, etc. The most important rule here is to keep like things together and to assign a permanent home. Baskets or bins can be used to house small items.

Seasonal items are great to store here. They are close at hand. It's more convenient storage than the basement for seldom-used gadgets and serving pieces.

Betty: "Let's get canisters off the kitchen counter and store flour, sugar, coffee, and tea in the pantry."

"I'm a teetotaler, so I never imbibe. I do have a weakness for Maraschino cherries, however, and have had some luck finding them in a bowl on the butler's pantry counter from time to time. It's a real sugar high and worth every empty calorie."

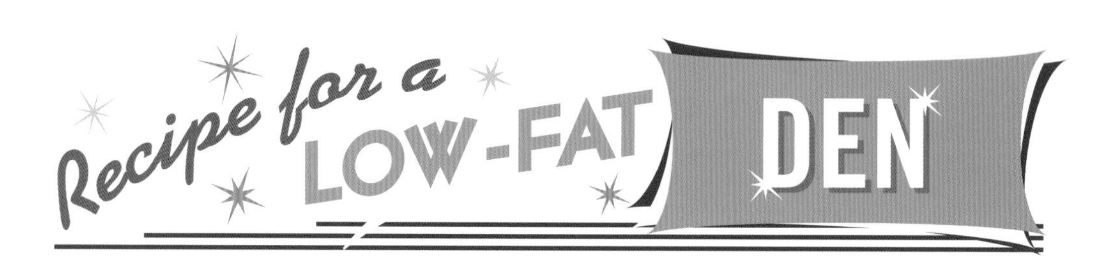

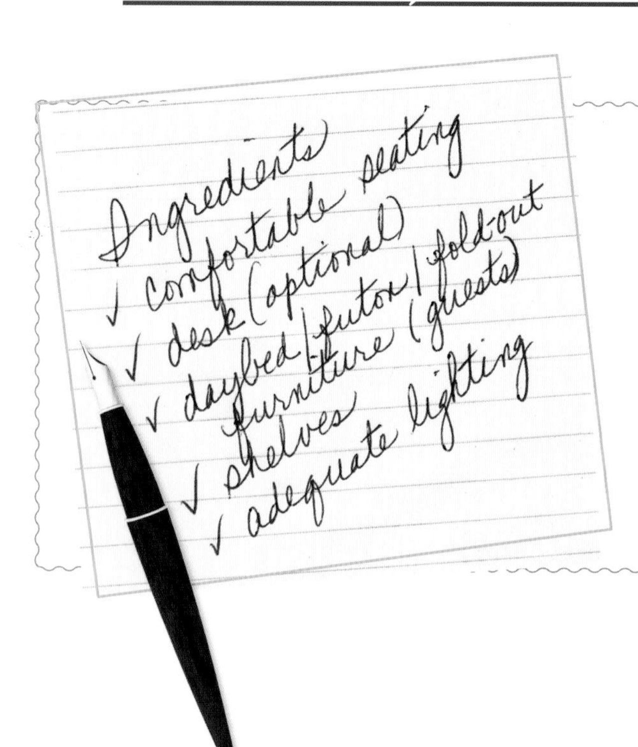

1. Take everything out of the room.
2. Paint, wash, or enjoy walls.
3. Replace or clean floor.
4. Identify focal point and room purpose.
5. Evaluate storage and lighting.
6. Replace with furniture for room's purpose.
7. Add art, accessories, and window treatment.
8. Relax and enjoy a good book.

Don't delay decisions!

If the den is a seldom-used room, it can attract random items from around the house. Don't let it be a holding area for delayed decisions.

It's all about atmosphere.

I envision cuddling up in a chair on a rainy day reading a good book here.

The den is usually a small room used as a:

- TV room.
- Playroom.
- Library.
- Office.
- Guest room.

Since this room hosts a variety of activities, it's important to keep storage a high priority. Shelves with labeled storage containers are preferred and can be a home to:

- Books.
- Guests' linens and toiletries.
- Office supplies.
- Toys and games.

If this room is used for several functions, consider furniture requirements. A library can double as a guest room with bookshelves, a writing desk, and a comfortable pullout sofa. Add a television and storage for toys, and kids can enjoy it as well.

If this room is used as an office: store paperwork in desk file drawers; a small filing cabinet for papers can also serve as a TV stand; 3-ring binders can be used to organize warranties and manuals in sheet protectors to keep on bookshelves; and lidded baskets or boxes can be used to house small, loose items.

Dens are usually small rooms so floor space is at a premium. When considering storage options, it's most efficient to use as much vertical space as possible. Bookshelves become a good choice. If there is no room for a TV stand, file cabinet, or nightstand, consider purchasing an entertainment center that's versatile enough for your storage needs.

> "This room is fun to scrounge around in looking for crumbs left by kids snacking while playing or watching TV. My favorite: a toss-up between Cheerios and Goldfish crackers. I'm also an avid reader, so I love the books left on the floor or end tables. My favorite: murder mysteries. Who can resist a good who-done-it?"

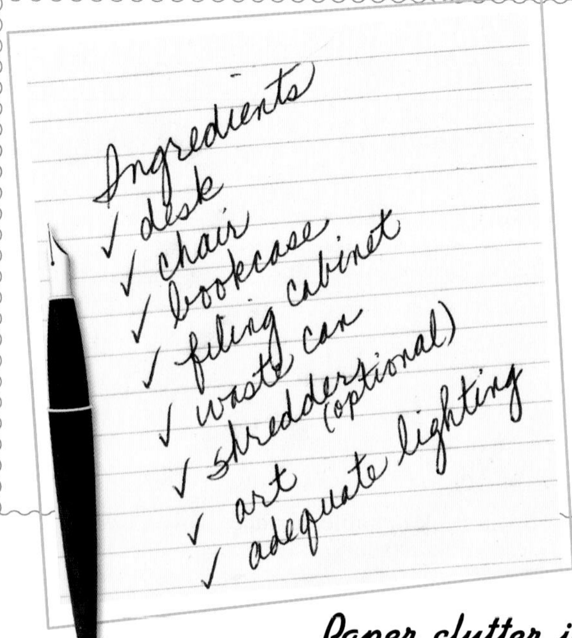

1. Take everything out of the room.
2. Paint, wash, or enjoy walls.
3. Replace or clean floor.
4. Ruthlessly go through all paperwork and files.
5. Evaluate filing system.
6. Shred or recycle unnecessary paper.
7. Eliminate extra furniture (filing cabinets/shelves).
8. Donate duplicates.
9. Evaluate lighting, art, accessories.
10. Enjoy your inspirational space.

Paper clutter is the most common form of clutter in a home.

Besides stray newspapers, mail, and magazines that become clutter throughout the house, the office is where all incoming papers collect.

It's your mind's playground.

Offices should be retreats where imagination and inspiration motivate us to accomplish great things, or just keep important papers organized and easily accessible.

Whether the home office is located in the kitchen, family room, den, living room, basement, or in its own dedicated room, the same rule applies: establish a home for all loose items and papers.

Betty: "This sounds simple, but many clients have stacks of papers piled on every surface and sometimes on the floor because the desk top is covered with a stapler, pens, post-it notes, calculator, tape dispenser, etc. I have them put all items in desk drawers or in a box/bin on a bookcase shelf. A great filing system is priceless to house all papers."

Barbara: "One of my pet peeves is seeing wires jumbled about under the desk and reaching toward the nearest outlet. I suggest bundling them in an orderly containment system (there are many available) and hiding them, if possible. A strategically positioned potted plant can hide wires between the desk and outlet. Plants clean the air and protect the environment from the negative ions emitted from electronic equipment. I also suggest keeping the shredder and trash can under the desk. I'm all about beauty wherever you can provide it, and an office is no exception."

When there is no home assigned for each type of paper that enters, miscellaneous piles appear on every surface including the floor.

The most important thing about keeping paper is being able to find it fast when you need it. The best filing tool I have found is a software program called the Paper Tiger. The system gives you an opportunity to type as many keywords you can think of to describe a file. It's like using a search engine to find a piece of paper you've filed.

All other office supplies or accessories should be kept off the desk or table surface. It's best when they are organized in little bins in desk drawers or in labeled boxes or bins on shelves. Remember: everything should have a permanent home.

"I have to admit I do love offices - so much paper, so little time. We mice are natural shredders you know. Once I got a brainstorm to make a hand print for my mom for Mother's Day. I chewed through the ink cartridge, dipped my paws in the ink and made handprints on a nice piece of paper. It was a good idea until I realized the ink took forever to dry, and I left a trail right back to my hiding space. Homeowner put a peanut butter trap there the next day. I had already sworn off the stuff, so I didn't go for it but it was sure hard to be around that heavenly aroma."

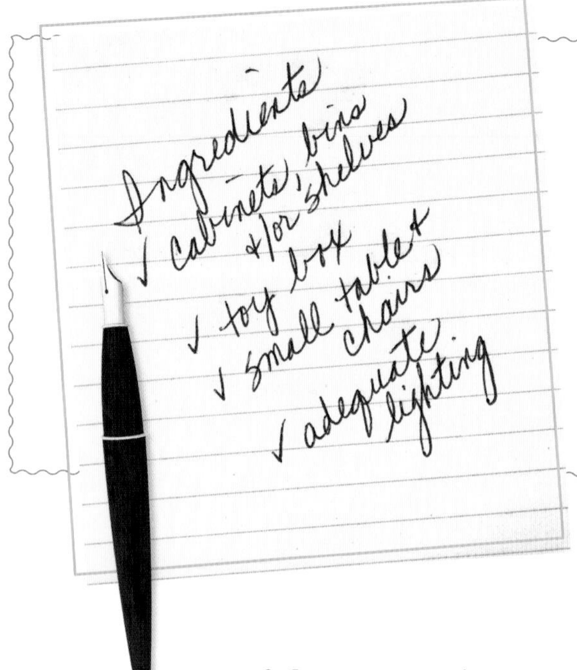

1. Take everything out of the room.
2. Paint, wash, or enjoy walls.
3. Replace or clean floor.
4. Evaluate storage/organization needs.
5. Install cabinets, shelves, bins, etc.
6. Fill donation bags/boxes.
7. Label bins/shelves and replace toys.
8. Let kids do next cleanup.

It's great when you can dedicate an entire room to toys!

I know toys and books are synonymous with raising kids, but even young moms appreciate the feeling of grown-up living areas. I salute clients who find clever storage containers like vintage suitcases to store toys and games and to house a neat stack of books.

It's fun to rotate your toys.

I love to convince clients to organize and store all toys in the basement playroom and rotate some to be enjoyed upstairs. This makes for quick cleanups.

To conquer toy overload:

- At birthdays and Christmas, have kids decide which toys they are willing to donate since they are receiving new ones. This will promote a generous spirit, making them cognizant of less-fortunate kids.
- Donate toys and books that kids have outgrown and are no longer age-appropriate. Discard broken toys or games with missing pieces.
- Keep toys stored in a dedicated space in the basement, rotating to the first floor for playtime. This keeps kids themselves from being overwhelmed with the volume of toys. Too many toys vying for attention make it hard to decide what to play with. Seeing so many out at one time makes cleanup look daunting.
- Purchase storage bins, tubs, toy boxes, or baskets to house on bookshelves. Label the shelves or containers in bedrooms and first floor play areas, keeping frequently-used ones on shelves within kids' reach. Keep similar types together.

Betty: "Kids actually enjoy an organized play space, especially when there is a labeled storage system within their reach. Bins and tubs are great for keeping like items together. When labeled, everything is easy to find and cleanup is quick and fun."

"Playrooms are fun for kids, but I don't get a kick out of them. I'm most interested in scavenging for little things I can use in my living space to enhance my lifestyle. Sometimes I chew through game boxes to find game pieces to use as accessories. Cool game tokens serve as sculptures on my end tables, like the ones from Parcheesi. I use checkers as chargers under my silver dime dinner plates for a festive touch. Stuffed animal fill works great for quilt batting. I do, however, love doll houses (great stuff sized just right). I have to admit that I sometimes sit in cool trucks and cars wishing I could take them for a spin. I am a guy after all."

1. Remove everything except appliances.
2. Paint, wash, or enjoy walls.
3. Replace or clean floor (under appliances too).
4. Evaluate lighting, window treatments, and storage needs.
5. Install cabinets/shelves/hooks.
6. Recycle or donate extras.
7. Add art and thinned out laundry supplies.
8. Enjoy an organized, spa-like laundry.

The dirt on laundry...

The smell on laundry day says clean. Laundry room clutter never says clean.

My favorite club without a membership...

Club soda can lift stains, and vodka can kill mold and mildew on fabrics. Or you can mix them, add a lemon zest and enjoy laundry day in a whole new way.

*L*aundry rooms, or combination laundry/mud rooms, attract stray items. Clothes, cleaning detergents, mops, brooms, buckets, brushes/sponges, light bulbs, batteries, watering cans, book bags, mail, and purses are typical items found in this room.

Storage is critical to corral all these items and provide permanent homes. Shelves or cabinets are your best choice. It's important to provide an area out of the reach of kids or pets. Having a home for laundry detergents keeps them off the top of the washer and dryer. They don't have to be moved every time you do laundry, and you'll have a clear surface for folding clothes.

Betty: "Cabinets are ideal because you can store like items in baskets or bins behind closed doors."

The laundry room is also a natural home for the ironing board. Ideally, it should be mounted on the wall or hung over the back of the door to keep it off the floor.

A rule of thumb in decluttering is to provide clear surfaces. In this case, the top of the washer and dryer should be clear. But don't forget the floor. It's also a surface. Find a home for buckets and mops (garage or basement) so that cleaning the floor is fast and easy.

Barbara: "I love to see a naked washer/dryer, sink, and a clear floor."

"If there's a litter box in this room, I steer clear. I can't stand the smell. I don't mind spending time in this room on laundry day though, when all the clothes are piled on the floor separated by color. It makes it easier for me when I need a specific fabric piece to complete my quilt. Once I chewed through a box of baking soda thinking it might be powdered sugar. Didn't taste as good but it really cleaned my teeth."

1. Take everything out of the room except bed/dressers.
2. Paint, wash, or enjoy walls.
3. Replace or clean floor.
4. Evaluate lighting, window treatments, and storage.
5. Remove excess furniture or non-bedroom items.
6. Make laundry home in closet, not sleeping area.
7. Incorporate art and accessories that are calming.
8. Enjoy a good night's rest.

A bedroom should be an oasis...

...for relaxation and sleep - calming, restful, and clutter-free.

I have strict rules for the bedroom.

All I want in my bedroom is a bed, dresser, mirror, candles, soft music, and fresh flowers.

It's amazing how clutter in a bedroom can sabotage relaxation. Even storage under the bed, though sight unseen, can prevent a good night's sleep.

Barbara: "I had a client that didn't want to see a clothes hamper in the room. She didn't want the visual reminder of laundry that needed to be done, so she slid laundry baskets full of dirty clothes under her bed. She complained of always waking up tired. I suggested she clear the shelf in her closet and place the laundry baskets there instead. She later told me she now wakes up refreshed since clearing out the area under her bed. The baskets in the closet keep all her clothes, clean and dirty, in one area."

Laundry is just one bedroom challenge. Kids' rooms also house toys, games, books, computers, and the occasional hamster cage or fish tank.

Betty : "I think we can relax on vacation because the bedrooms away from home are so sparse."

To minimize distractions that prevent us from relaxing, all essential items should be organized and stored in the closet, dressers, or cabinets. When there is a specific home for everything even kids can keep their rooms clean.

"I like to hang out in bedrooms of people who eat in their bed while watching TV. I feast on the crumbs, and there are always crumbs. Sometimes I get lucky and kids will hide their candy in the desk or dresser drawers. Like a flimsy candy wrapper is going to keep me from chocolate. I don't think so. There's usually pieces and parts of toys, games, and a stash of hamster food. I chew out old, stained underwear that's lying around and keep the pieces to make a quilt. Before I leave, I tease the hamster with hamster wheel jokes. OK, so I do two cruel things."

Recipe for a LOW-FAT BASEMENT

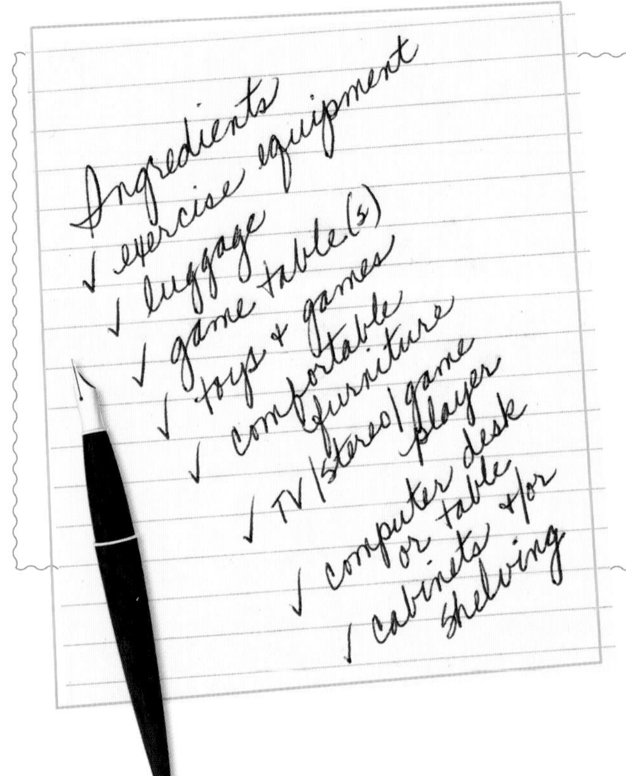

1. Take everything out, one area at a time.
2. Separate into bins for trash, recycle, donate, and relocate.
3. Paint/clean walls and vacuum cobwebs.
4. Replace/clean floor.
5. Evaluate storage and living needs.
6. Install cabinets, shelves, bins.
7. Implement areas for hobbies, relaxing, games, storage.
8. Enjoy your newfound space.

There's living area down there!

If you have a basement, don't abuse it with clutter. Maximize storage and use the rest for living areas.

It's my alternative social spot.

I love theme basements. A sports bar or diner are right up my alley.

*B*asements can be a catchall for everything that doesn't fit upstairs. When you don't have an attic or garage, it becomes a glorified storage unit. It's easy to lose or forget items hiding here.

One of Barbara's unforgettable basement design jobs involved so much clutter that mold was covering the carpet, walls, furniture, clothes, papers, and everything in between. "The homeowner put everything in the basement she didn't know what to do with. We found items inherited from her deceased relatives mixed in with their bulk food, paper products, a dog crate, family pictures in bags (not in photo albums), gifts unopened, new items in packaging with receipts attached, camping equipment, luggage, seasonal decorations, gift wrapping supplies, craft supplies, many dried flower arrangements, vases and baskets, etc. I wasted no time in calling to have a dumpster delivered. We ended up filling three dumpsters before we were able to start cleaning, repairing, and remodeling."

If items had been placed in cabinets or on shelves, they would not have been destroyed by mold. Once the basement was cleared, new flooring and ceiling tiles were installed. Walls, trim, and doors were painted.

Air circulation is important in the typically damp environment of basements. This basement required two dehumidifiers – one dedicated to the crawl space, and the other to serve the living areas.

This basement project ended up providing a cozy family room, kitchen, craft room, game room, and back storage/furnace room. Family photos were put in albums with some framed and hung on walls or displayed in bookcases. Tools, Christmas decorations, and games are now organized and stored. The family now enjoys 1200 square feet of new living space.

"Basements are made for mouse adventures. I've stolen dog food from the kitchen dog bowl and hidden my stash under the sofa in the basement. I've played and slept in the doll house. I've chewed insulation to make a comfy nest under the stairs. I've chewed through the Monopoly game box to play with the silver dog. I've even had a close call trying to get peanut butter off a mousetrap. My arm got caught when it snapped. I made such a loud noise flipping it back and forth in the ceiling that Homeowner had to cancel his vacation flight because he didn't want to leave me like that. He released me, and I ran for my life (literally). I've sworn off peanut butter. I know it's a good protein, but I'll settle for dog food."

1. Remove everything that isn't exercise equipment.
2. Paint, wash, or enjoy walls.
3. Replace or clean floor.
4. Donate unused equipment.
5. Evaluate lighting and window treatments.
6. Incorporate art/mirrors and television.
7. Allow enough floor space for routines.
8. If you love your space you'll work out more.

Owning exercise equipment isn't enough to get you in shape.
Don't use it? Donate.

Exercise doesn't have to be lonely.

To stay in shape, I enjoy a good workout - especially with the right partner.

*U*nless you're an athlete or disciplined workout freak, this is the least used room, or area, of the home. Dedicated exercise areas are always set up with good intentions. Neglected areas attract clutter, and this room is commonly neglected. Inaccessible exercise equipment that is piled with other things is taking up valuable space and becomes clutter. If you don't use the equipment, sell or donate it.

Betty: "I've had clients that needed to start fresh and acknowledge that it's freeing to get rid of old, unused equipment that produced feelings of guilt."

Barbara: "Exercise equipment is not glamorous. It should all be contained in one room, not scattered about the house."

Suggestions for an exercise area or room:

- Paint the room vibrant, fun colors, and add art or mirrors.
- Carpeting or an area rug will make floor routines more comfortable.
- Keep all exercise equipment, including workout books, notes, DVD's, weights, balls, bands, mats, kettle bells, etc., in the exercise area.
- A television is good to play workout DVD's, watch workout shows, or just have on as a companion or distraction.
- Music is a plus for motivation. A surface near an electrical outlet comes in handy for music players.
- It's helpful to have a surface for a water bottle as well.
- Keep all non-workout related items out of this area.
- It's easy to let storage items, ironing, unfinished sewing or craft projects, etc., creep into this area. A cluttered exercise area will discourage you from working out. If you don't have a dedicated laundry or sewing/craft area, create room in a closet for the ironing board, sewing machine and supplies. Like items organized and labeled in clear, plastic containers are easily found when needed.

> "As I mentioned in my introduction letter, I do work out. I fast-walk, run, do Yoga, and use the bouncy-ball for ab crunches. That keeps me in shape, and I don't need a dedicated room to do it in. I store my bouncy-ball in a corner of the family room and get it out when Homeowner watches film noir movies."

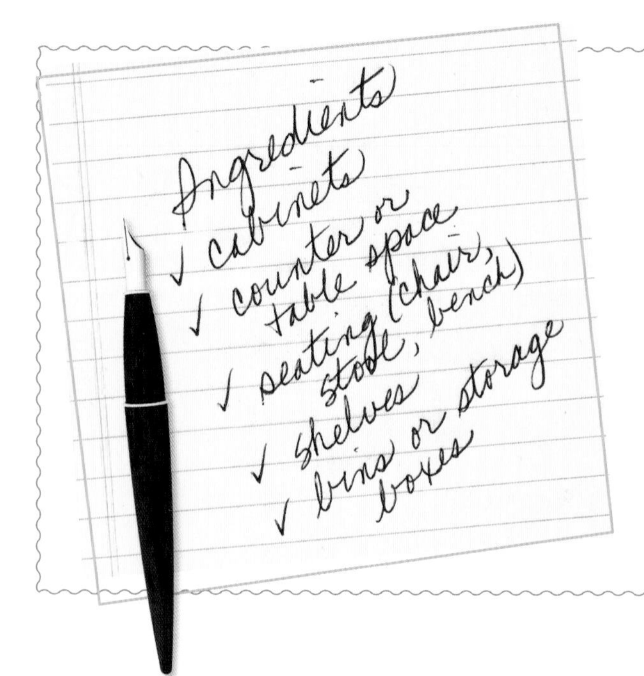

1. Take everything out of the room.
2. Paint, wash, or enjoy the walls.
3. Replace or clean the floor.
4. Evaluate lighting, window treatments, and storage needs.
5. Install and label cabinets, shelves, and bins.
6. Ruthlessly eliminate unnecessary project material.
7. Recycle or donate to schools.
8. Put away only current projects.
9. Enjoy sharing your talent with others in your new room.

It's easy to get bombarded with an abundance of sewing and craft supplies. Schools would just love your extras!

I like to have room to move.

When people ask me if I sew, I reply, "Only when I have to mend a gown." I need plenty of space, and a cluttered sewing area just won't do.

*T*o maximize efficiency:

- Have a table top surface for a sewing machine or craft area, leaving sufficient empty work space.
- Chair should be kept clear. Do not pile laundry, ironing, or sewing projects here.
- Shelves, cabinets, or open bins should be labeled, keeping like items together. Clear, plastic, shoebox-sized, lidded containers are best.
- Donate all extra supplies, and discard unfinished projects that won't get done.

This room is a challenge to organize and declutter because of the volume of small items that need to be sorted, categorized, and stored. It is important to take the time to do this project, however, because it will enable you to find what you need quickly.

Many people have duplicate sewing or craft supplies because they can never find them. Save stress and money by going through everything. You'll find things you haven't seen in a long time, identify duplicates, and free yourself of all the unwanted, unfinished work that drains your energy.

"OK, this is my favorite room in the house for finding things to repurpose. I use yarn and dowel sticks to "rope off" areas in the attic where I don't want other critters to go. It doesn't work with the squirrels. They're so high and mighty they just go wherever they please with no consideration for my space.

Thimbles make great chairs, pompoms perfect throw pillows, fabric swatches great throws and blankets, and thread spools trendy end tables. The possibilities are endless. I go for the shabby chic, vintage look - not exactly Pottery Barn, but it's home."

1. Take everything out of the attic.
2. Evaluate insulation, safety of floor, lighting.
3. Install hooks and/or shelves.
4. Recycle or donate unused, unwanted, or neglected items.
5. Obtain plastic bins with lids and label kept items.
6. Move around freely in your new space.

Find everything a home.

One thing to keep in mind for attic storage: it does get hot. Candles or items sensitive to heat should not be stored there.

It's a hassle climbing attic stairs in heels...

...but it's worth it to keep things stored off the main floors.

Since this area is out of sight and mind, it's easy for items to find permanent homes and become forgotten until it's time to move. This area can usually stand to lose weight.

There are endless possibilities for items that can be stored in the attic, but this is a recipe for an attic on a diet. If you don't have sufficient closet, garage, or basement storage, the attic is a good alternative for storing luggage, camping supplies, baby furniture for a still-growing family, scraps of carpeting, sports equipment, etc.

It's important to store items in moisture-proof containers with lids. Clear, plastic bins or tubs are best for this environment. You can easily see what's inside, especially if you label them clearly.

For speedy identification, some plastic storage containers sport seasonal colors: red and green for Christmas, orange and black for Halloween, etc. These are fun, festive, and very functional when you want to arrange areas by how often and when they require access.

Make sure to open all taped boxes that may have been moved from home to home. You may find mold and mildew-damaged items that need to be discarded, especially if they haven't been opened in many years.

Attics shouldn't house neglected items because there's room for them. Many attics are filled with discarded furniture or trunks of grandma's clothes that are not even worth donating. If there's sentimentality attached to these objects, take a picture for your photo album and discard or recycle.

"Attics are one of the most popular hangouts for mice and squirrels. I hate sharing space with squirrels. They are so high-brow. They're cute, and they know it - probably the best looking of the rodent family - very playful and love to tease. Try living with that type of roommate: a high-energy, good-looking, arrogant, practical joker."

Recipe for a LOW-FAT CRAWL SPACE

1. Take everything out.
2. Evaluate condition of floor and lighting.
3. Recycle or donate unused, unwanted, or neglected items.
4. Label clear, plastic bins with lids and fill with kept items.
5. Enjoy finding things quickly.

Squeeze in there!

Some crawl spaces are difficult to access. Because of this they rarely get cleaned out. Don't let that happen to you.

I prefer long, elbow-length gloves.

I hate getting on my hands and knees in these tight, moist spaces – don't want to ruin my clothes or scuff my heels. I prefer to keep storage at a minimum and at an arm's reach here.

Crawl spaces are great when they have a cement floor. Dirt and/or gravel spaces are moist, which limits storage options. Use heavy-ply plastic layered on the surface with a dedicated dehumidifier to control moisture.

Mold and mildew damage is a concern in crawl spaces. Storing items in clear plastic tubs with lids is best for protection against moisture. Label contents to store and find them quickly and easily.

Betty: "Some clients have had to destroy tax records, cancelled checks, and books due to mold and mildew damage in moist crawl spaces where they were stored."

This is not the place for photo boxes, photo albums, art, framed prints, clothing, stuffed animals, or anything that is sensitive to high humidity or moisture. Be very selective in what you store in this area.

If you have valuable collectibles that are stored in original packaging, do not store here. Cardboard packaging is especially susceptible to mold and mildew. You won't be able to sell them with mold-stained boxes. Find another storage location, or get them out to enjoy, sell, or donate now before they have a chance to become damaged.

"Mice love warm, moist spaces filled with clutter. They are so homey and welcoming. Crawl spaces are one of our favorite places to call home. Boxes and old papers are great to shred for bedding."

Ingredients
- ✓ weather-resistant furniture
- ✓ durable table(s)
- ✓ potted plants (optional)

1. Take everything out of the room.
2. Paint, wash, or enjoy walls.
3. Replace or clean floor.
4. Evaluate lighting and window treatments.
5. Incorporate minimum of furniture.
6. Add art and accessories.
7. Make some lemonade, sit back, and enjoy the view.

This room is a luxury. Don't abuse it by making it into a storage unit.

Florida, or somewhere even better...

This room is made for relaxing and imagining being surrounded by palm trees, an ocean breeze, and a good-looking cabana boy serving umbrella drinks.

*T*his space is the bridge between the house and outdoors. When comfortably furnished inside and landscaped neatly outside, it provides an oasis for mini-vacation living.

Sometimes serving as a playroom, this room can coexist with adult entertainment when closed storage for toys and games is provided.

Clear out everything except:

- Comfortable seating.
- Coffee and/or end tables.
- Adequate lighting. Floor lamps for reading.
- Storage for television/toys/games/books/bar essentials.
- Area rug, art (wall space permitting), and accessories.
- Potted plants (live or artificial).

This room is usually off the family room, great room, or kitchen, so it is visible from the main living areas. Clutter accumulation, or long-term storage, keeps you from enjoying this valuable real estate.

This room was planned to be used for luxury living, a way to live like you're on vacation, not to store clutter. We don't live with clutter on vacation. Don't settle for it here.

> "I've spent many vacations in screened porches. Don't forget that we mice have sharp incisor teeth that can chew through just about anything, including screens. If we need to get in out of the elements, it's a mighty inviting room, especially if it's filled with clutter, offering many places to hide."

1. Take everything out of the garage.
2. Separate necessities from items to donate, recycle, or sell.
3. Install cabinets, shelves, bins, or hooks as needed.
4. Find a home for everything, placing similar things together.
5. Park your car in your new, clutter-free garage.

The best way to tackle the garage...

...is to take everything out and have it painted. Scheduling a painter expedites the project. Then you can go through everything and discard old, useless, or misplaced items you forgot you had. “The keepers” can then be stored in cabinets, bins, or shelves along the walls.

Why would anyone park on the street?

I’ve had clients that couldn’t park their cars in the garage because it was filled with so much stuff. A $60,000 car was exposed to the elements while their accumulated junk was warm and dry.

*G*arages are built to house cars. Using it as a storage unit and leaving your car outside is hard on your car. The sun alone is very damaging to the paint. If you live in a cold climate in the winter, it's just not fun to have to scrape your windows every time you want to leave. Your car will hold its value longer if kept protected.

Typical garage clutter:

- Fun stuff: bicycles, toys, sporting goods, golf clubs, golf carts, go-carts, 4-wheelers, motorcycles, wagons, sleds, inline skates, ice skates, etc.
- Garden stuff: wheelbarrow, tool carts, rakes, shovels, edgers, trimmers, garden sheers, pots, potting soil, pesticides, fertilizer, spreader, lawn mower, leaf blower, snow blower, bird seed, etc.
- Tool stuff: too many to mention, some scattered about on a work table.
- Car stuff: car covers, car washing buckets, sponges, drying cloths, soaps, waxes, wheel cleaners, etc.
- House stuff: discarded building supplies from the last remodel, anything that won't fit in the house.
- Seasonal stuff: artificial Christmas tree, variety of wreaths for front door, Christmas lights, holiday décor for inside and outside, tiki torches, patio furniture, seasonal lawn ornaments, etc.
- Boxes of miscellaneous storage.

When you take everything out, you will find duplicates and things you didn't even know you had. You will be able to discard or donate what you no longer use. You can categorize and organize the items you love and need into appropriate storage areas.

Your reward for tackling this room will be the space you've created for your car. You will also know what you have and be able to find it quickly.

> "Don't forget to put bird food, pet food, grass seed, etc., in heavy, plastic containers with tight-fitting lids. We mice just can't help ourselves when these items are easily accessible. :)"

Recipe for a LOW-FAT DECK PATIO

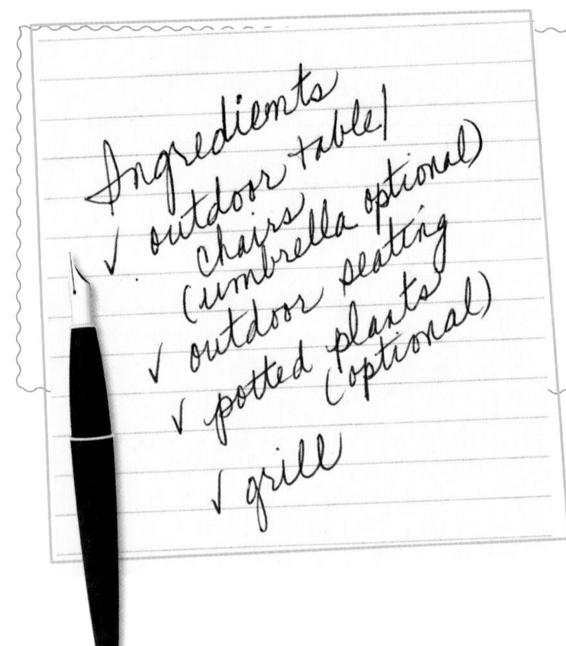

1. Take everything off the deck or patio.
2. Paint, stain, or clean surface.
3. Evaluate outdoor lighting.
4. Incorporate grill and minimum of furniture.
5. Invite people over for a cookout.

Think reuse for outdoors!

Furniture will be exposed to the elements and may be prone to rust. A fresh coat of Rustoleum or similar type paint will bring new life to old pieces.

A wonderful place to relax.

Give me a drink, and let me sit around with friends while I smell the steak and shrimp cooking on the grill.

Typical deck or patio clutter:

- Pots filled with dirt or a dying plant.
- Too much furniture (chairs and side tables).
- Large, outdoor toys.
- Pet bowls.
- Bags of bird food.
- Cushions for furniture.
- Turkey deep fryer.
- Seasonal discards (Christmas tree, pumpkins, etc.).
- Grill.

This area can be a real treat to relax in. Clutter can inhibit relaxation.

Fill empty pots with seasonal plants. Give up on dying plants and replace with live ones. Discard old, broken, or unneeded items. Donate extras. Find permanent homes for outdoor toys (garage or shed) and bird food. Store furniture cushions in shed or garage to keep them from the elements. They will not only stay cleaner, but will be protected from mold and mildew. Store the turkey deep fryer (once cooled, of course) in garage or shed. Christmas trees can be mulched or placed in the back of the yard for a critter sanctuary. Pumpkins can be left in the back of the yard to be kicked open and eaten by deer or discarded.

Barbara: "There are clients of mine that are hard-core entertainers and love spontaneous social gatherings. On the driveway leading to their patio, they haul out tables, chairs, an outdoor rug, and torches from the garage when they want neighbors to stop by for a chat and glass of wine. They even host Friday Night Flicks complete with lawn chairs set up theatre-style. Movies are projected on a screen. It's like a drive-in movie without the cars. Needless to say, these clients have become my best friends."

"I have never been invited to these parties, but I've crashed a few. I hang out in the garage next to the bag of grass seed (a mouse staple, believe it or not) and dart out for an occasional dropped piece of popcorn or Reese's peanut butter cup - peanut butter and chocolate. Now that's worth risking my life over!"

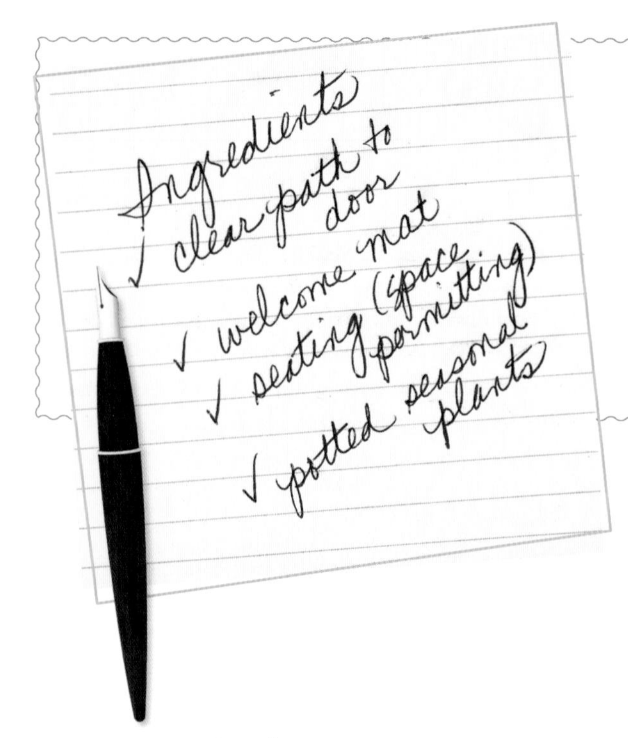

1. Take everything off the porch.
2. Paint or clean the surface.
3. Evaluate outdoor lighting, house numbers, and mailbox.
4. Incorporate outdoor door mat, furniture, and planters.
5. Invite your neighbors over for a cool drink.

Welcome!

The porch is the welcome mat of the house. If it's cluttered or dirty, it doesn't give visitors an open, warm reception.

Rock and swing...

I love porches that are large enough to house rockers or porch swings. My favorite indulgence is sitting on a porch rocker, watching the world go by. Nothing beats sipping a cold drink on the porch with friends or family members.

Porch clutter is there for the whole world to see. Excess clutter could even become a hazard and obstruct access to doors. Toys, skates, or other debris can be tripped over, causing serious injuries.

The porch is another area meant for relaxation and social gathering. It is also an extension of the yard. If the porch is used for storage, or just collects toys, gardening projects, etc., it may be due for a good weeding.

If you're not using the items in the house or yard, they might be unnecessary. Don't let the porch become a landing station for things you don't want to deal with. They should be returned to their permanent homes, discarded, or donated.

Ideally, a porch shouldn't have anything but seating and seasonal potted plants accented with a clean door mat and adequate lighting. Cobwebs and bugs that collect in your outdoor fixtures also represent clutter and deferred maintenance.

To look best, a porch should have:

- No clutter.
- Surface swept and cobwebs cleaned.
- Repairs made to steps and/or handrail.
- Peeling surfaces scraped and painted.
- House numbers large enough to be seen from the street.

"Many of my mouse friends that live in the South boast of porch living year-round. What could be better than pet lovers who are thoughtful enough to put food and water on the porch? Add an upholstered sofa and life couldn't be more grand."

1. Remove everything from the yard.
2. Remove overgrown or dead trees, bushes, or plants.
3. Trim, edge, weed, and cut lawn.
4. Discard excess lawn ornaments.
5. Recycle or donate all outgrown lawn toys.
6. Incorporate seasonal plants and enjoy.

It's the first spot for clutter!

When people look at houses, the first thing they notice is the yard. Too much personal expression (lawn ornaments) can turn off visitors or prospective buyers and be considered clutter.

A purposeful, personal touch can be fun!

Since I love everything vintage, pink flamingos in the yard are OK by me.

*N*eighbors and passersby all see the yard and every toy, bike, and lawn ornament in it. We've become a side door/garage door society, rarely entering our own house through the front, yet this is where our guests first experience our home. A low-fat yard should be void of not only objects, but weeds, fallen fruit, overgrown landscape, and peeling paint.

Betty: "I tell clients, especially if they plan to sell their house, that people judge a book by its cover. Their impression is, 'If the yard isn't clean, the house must not be either'"

Yards can also be dumping grounds for scraps of construction wood, bricks, stones, old or broken toys, garden equipment, pots filled with dirt or dead plants, gas cans, broken appliances, cars that no longer run, trash cans, and recycle bins.

Discard everything ruined by the elements. Donate everything else not needed or loved, and store like things together, preferably out of sight. If there is a permanent home for the trash can/recycle bin and garden equipment, they can all be returned for fast and easy cleanup.

Once everything is cleaned, cleared, weeded, and trimmed it's time to consider adequate lighting and visible house numbers. Visitors can't find your house if it's not clearly marked. Realtors are surprised when homeowners put their house on the market without house numbers that are easy to read from the street. If people can't find your house, they can't buy it!

Barbara: "Friends can't find it for parties either!"

"If you don't want mice, squirrels, chipmunks, raccoons, and moles making their homes in your yard, be diligent at picking up fruit that falls from trees. Most fellow rodents don't mind a bruise or two, but I steer clear from fallen fruit."

1. Take everything out of the shed.
2. Repair walls, doors, and floor if needed.
3. Sweep out debris.
4. Install hooks or shelves if possible.
5. Recycle old, rusted, or damaged items.
6. Donate unneeded or unwanted items.
7. Incorporate bagged items into clear, plastic, lidded containers.
8. Install a lock for safety.

Out of sight?

Some neighborhoods don't allow storage sheds. I love those neighborhoods. Sheds can be an eyesore and encourage clutter.

I prefer to shed the shed.

I'm all about glamour and I don't find a bit of glamour in sheds. I avoid them like the plague.

Sheds should be kept maintained to protect possessions from the elements. Metal sheds can rust and so can their contents.

Sheds are commonly used to store bicycles, wheelbarrows, garden tools, etc., that are also prone to rust. Preferred are insulated, air-tight, wooden sheds to protect these and other similar items.

Installing shelves will help maximize storage capacity and keep hazardous items out of the reach of kids and pets.

Barbara: "I had a client who stored an open bag of pesticides in the shed. Her son's playmate went in there to retrieve a ball that rolled next to the bag. That exposure was enough to send him to the ER. He became temporarily paralyzed in his legs from inhaling the fumes and getting residue on his hands. Fortunately, he recovered. It's very important to keep harmful toxins sealed in their original containers and out of the reach of kids and pets."

Bird seed and fertilizer are other popular shed items sold in bags. These bags are best stored in clear, plastic, lidded containers. This protects them from the elements and rodents looking for a free lunch.

"I remember friends telling me they had a great party setup in a backyard shed. Lots of plastic bags to shred, places to hide behind, bird food to eat, protection from the elements, and privacy to party at all hours - until Homeowner got tired of them scattering every time he opened the door. He started leaving the shed door open all the time. That put such a damper on their parties that they finally moved on. It didn't bother me a bit. I was never invited to their parties anyway."

ABOUT THE AUTHOR

Sharon Kreighbaum owns an interior design and staging firm. Her love for everything vintage inspired her to build an authentic 50's diner in her basement. She enjoys wearing vintage clothing, shoes, and accessories. She has a passion for helping people and houses lose weight by eliminating clutter. Sharon is planning a nationwide book tour to teach the benefits of the house diet and to provide material for the next book in the series - "Is Your Closet Overweight?"

Sharon is married with three children and resides in Hudson, Ohio. She lives like she's on vacation, enjoying luxury with the barest of essentials.

BOOK CLUB DISCUSSION QUESTIONS

1. The author uses fictional characters to offer insights and advice throughout the book. Barbara focuses on relationships and beauty. Betty focuses on organization, efficiency, and cleanliness. Bob speaks from a mouse's point of view on his way of dealing with clutter. Who do you identify with? Why is that aspect of your house most important to you?

2. The Staged Makeovers Diet encourages getting rid of everything you don't need and giving it to others. Is it easier to go through your house looking for things to give when you know someone can really use them? Does it make you feel good knowing you've helped a disaster victim, battered woman, or single mother start over?

3. Do you feel you can't let things go unless you know who is getting them? Does this keep you from donating to charities? Is this an excuse to hold on to items?

4. You can recycle papers/plastics/cardboard/glass/metals, but did you know that you are recycling when you donate, buy used, or repurpose what you already own? Do you feel your recycling efforts make a difference in the world?

5. There is a movement to living smaller and more simply. Cohousing communities are sprouting up around the United States and Europe. Denmark led the way by building cluster houses with shared spaces for activities and communal meals in a common house. The benefits are close, meaningful relationships with neighbors who learn from and support one another. Their motto is to live with less and share with others. Do you see this movement continuing to grow?

6. Another popular trend to living smaller is to build miniature houses – small, portable houses that are affordable – less than the cost of a room addition. People who choose these structures want to pare down their possessions, consume less, value quality over quantity, and live simple and small. "You start to peel away the things that are unnecessary," says Gregory Johnson, cofounder of the Small House Society. "It helps you define your priorities with regard to your material things." (Naples Daily News, Sunday, 12/5/10, 9F) Do you see this as yet another movement to living with less for a more fulfilling life?

7. To live in a low-fat house you will save money by not buying unnecessary items, duplicates or commercial cleaning products, receiving tax breaks for donations, repurposing what you already own, and eliminating storage expense. Is saving money incentive enough to encourage you to put your house on a diet?

8. A low-fat house improves relationships (less stressful environment, less spending), health (less toxic, cleaner, more spacious, controlled environment reduces depression), money (saved in reduced buying, donation tax break, repurposing what you own, homemade cleansers), and time (saved in locating items, less shopping and cleaning tasks streamlined). How can you benefit by putting your house on a diet?

9. An abundance of clutter is usually the result of an addiction to spending, difficulty organizing/letting things go, and associating things with your identity. Do you experience a rush or high when getting a bargain? Do you shop when bored, upset, or as a reward? Do you associate things with memories or your status? Do you have a hard time deciding where to put things for fear you won't remember where they are?

10. People who have lots of clutter are often overweight themselves. Things and food are used to fill emotional voids. Do you find yourself eating when bored, upset, or as a reward?

11. Passive rebellion toward an unhappy marriage can be seen by excessive shopping, not cleaning, or overeating. Do you see how this can lead to clutter or weight gain?

12. Having someone declutter or organize with you is best. That person can be objective and encourage you to make good decisions. Is there a friend or family member you can share this experience with?

13. Are some of your favorite memories from vacations? Would you like to live like you're on vacation? How can you change your house to be more like vacation living?

14. A popular design mantra is, "Less is more." How can you change the way you decorate to reflect this principle?

15. How do you feel about adapting Betty's cleaning routine? Do you see yourself saving money by cleaning with vinegar, baking soda, and lemon oil? Does it help you to know how long it takes to clean a room? Do you dread cleaning because you feel it will take too long?

16. Are you surprised to see how many pounds and inches can be lost when getting rid of items? Do you like this measurable approach to experiencing success in living a low-fat life?